BLACK AND SMOKELESS POWDERS

Technologies for Finding Bombs and the Bomb Makers

Committee on Smokeless and Black Powder

Board on Chemical Sciences and Technology
Commission on Physical Sciences, Mathematics, and Applications

National Research Council

NATIONAL ACADEMY PRESS
Washington, D.C.   1998

NOTICE: The project that is the subject of this report was approved by the Governing Board of the National Research Council, whose members are drawn from the councils of the National Academy of Sciences, the National Academy of Engineering, and the Institute of Medicine. The members of the committee responsible for the report were chosen for their special competences and with regard for appropriate balance.

The National Academy of Sciences is a private, nonprofit, self-perpetuating society of distinguished scholars engaged in scientific and engineering research, dedicated to the furtherance of science and technology and to their use for the general welfare. Upon the authority of the charter granted to it by the Congress in 1863, the Academy has a mandate that requires it to advise the federal government on scientific and technical matters. Dr. Bruce Alberts is president of the National Academy of Sciences.

The National Academy of Engineering was established in 1964, under the charter of the National Academy of Sciences, as a parallel organization of outstanding engineers. It is autonomous in its administration and in the selection of its members, sharing with the National Academy of Sciences the responsibility for advising the federal government. The National Academy of Engineering also sponsors engineering programs aimed at meeting national needs, encourages education and research, and recognizes the superior achievements of engineers. Dr. William A. Wulf is president of the National Academy of Engineering.

The Institute of Medicine was established in 1970 by the National Academy of Sciences to secure the services of eminent members of appropriate professions in the examination of policy matters pertaining to the health of the public. The Institute acts under the responsibility given to the National Academy of Sciences by its congressional charter to be an adviser to the federal government and, upon its own initiative, to identify issues of medical care, research, and education. Dr. Kenneth I. Shine is president of the Institute of Medicine.

The National Research Council was organized by the National Academy of Sciences in 1916 to associate the broad community of science and technology with the Academy's purposes of furthering knowledge and advising the federal government. Functioning in accordance with general policies determined by the Academy, the Council has become the principal operating agency of both the National Academy of Sciences and the National Academy of Engineering in providing services to the government, the public, and the scientific and engineering communities. The Council is administered jointly by both Academies and the Institute of Medicine. Dr. Bruce Alberts and Dr. William A. Wulf are chairman and vice chairman, respectively, of the National Research Council.

This study was supported by Contract No. TATF-96-17 between the National Academy of Sciences and the Department of the Treasury. Any opinions, findings, conclusions, or recommendations expressed in this publication are those of the author(s) and do not necessarily reflect the view of the organizations or agencies that provided support for this project.

Library of Congress Catalog Card Number 98-87764
International Standard Book Number 0-309-06246-2

Additional copies of this report are available from:
National Academy Press
2101 Constitution Avenue, N.W.
Box 285
Washington, DC 20055
800-624-6242
202-334-3313 (in the Washington metropolitan area)
http://www.nap.edu

COMMITTEE ON SMOKELESS AND BLACK POWDER

EDWIN P. PRZYBYLOWICZ , Eastman Kodak Company (retired), *Chair*
MARGARET A. BERGER, Brooklyn Law School
ALEXANDER BEVERIDGE, Royal Canadian Mounted Police
LEO R. GIZZI, Consultant, Christiansburg, Virginia
JANICE M. HIROMS, Consultant, Crosby, Texas
KARL V. JACOB, The Dow Chemical Company
CHARLES PARMENTER, Indiana University
PER-ANDERS PERSSON, New Mexico Institute of Mining and Technology
WALTER F. ROWE, George Washington University
ROGER L. SCHNEIDER, Rho Sigma Associates, Inc.
RONALD L. SIMMONS, Naval Surface Warfare Center, U.S. Navy
JUDITH BANNON SNOW, Los Alamos National Laboratory
RONALD R. VANDEBEEK, Natural Resources Canada
RAYMOND S. VOORHEES, U.S. Postal Inspection Service

Liaisons, Board on Chemical Sciences and Technology

JOHN J. WISE, Mobil Research and Development Corporation (retired)
BARBARA J. GARRISON, Pennsylvania State University

Project Staff

ELIZABETH L. GROSSMAN, Program Officer
CHRISTOPHER K. MURPHY, Program Officer
GREG EYRING, Consultant
DAVID GRANNIS, Project Assistant

Preface

The Committee on Smokeless and Black Powder (see Appendix A) was appointed by the National Research Council (NRC) in response to the mandate in the Antiterrorism and Effective Death Penalty Act of 1996 to address two basic areas: (1) the feasibility of adding tracer elements to smokeless and black powder for the purpose of detection and (2) the feasibility of adding tracer elements to smokeless and black powder for the purpose of identification. (See Appendix B for a detailed statement of task.) As part of these tasks, the committee considered potential risks to human life or safety, utility for law enforcement, effects on the quality and performance of the powders for their intended lawful use, potential effects on the environment, cost-effectiveness, and susceptibility to countermeasures in the evaluation of markers and taggants.

The study focused on science and technology issues related to detecting bombs and identifying bombers, with the goal of framing the issues and furnishing a report that provides a clear description of the technical options that exist to limit the threat from bombings that use smokeless or black powder. This report presents the committee's conclusions and recommendations and provides advice to officials of the Bureau of Alcohol, Tobacco, and Firearms on which to base recommendations to Congress.

In its initial meetings (Appendix C), the committee received a number of briefings that are summarized in Appendixes D and E. The committee is grateful to the individuals who provided technical information and insight during these briefings. This information helped to provide a sound foundation on which the committee was able to base its work. The committee solicited input from the scientific community and affected stakeholders on the issues delineated in the committee's charge and considered all such sources of information throughout the study.

This study was conducted under the auspices of the NRC's Board on Chemical Sciences and Technology and its staff. The committee acknowledges this support. The chair is particularly grateful to the members of this committee, who worked diligently and effectively on a demanding schedule to produce this report.

Edwin P. Przybylowicz, *Chair*
Committee on Smokeless and Black Powder

Acknowledgment of Reviewers

This report has been reviewed by individuals chosen for their diverse perspectives and technical expertise, in accordance with procedures approved by the National Research Council's (NRC's) Report Review Committee. The purpose of this independent review is to provide candid and critical comments that will assist the authors and the NRC in making the published report as sound as possible and to ensure that the report meets institutional standards for objectivity, evidence, and responsiveness to the study charge. The contents of the review comments and draft manuscript remain confidential to protect the integrity of the deliberative process. We wish to thank the following individuals for their participation in the review of this report:

Randy Becker, Los Angeles Police Department,
Paul W. Cooper, Sandia National Laboratories (retired),
Paul B. Ferrara, Virginia Division of Forensic Science,
W. Carl Lineberger, University of Colorado,
Lyle O. Malotky, Federal Aviation Administration,
David W. McCall, AT&T Bell Laboratories (retired),
Neale A. Messina, Princeton Combustion Research Laboratories,
Roy R. Miller, United Technology,
Hyla S. Napadensky, Napadensky Energetics, Inc. (retired),
Harrison Shull, U.S. Naval Postgraduate School (retired),
Peter J. Stang, University of Utah,
Frank H. Stillinger, Bell Laboratories, and
Patrick H. Windham, Windham Consulting.

Although the individuals listed above provided many constructive comments and suggestions, responsibility for the final content of this report rests solely with the authoring committee and the NRC.

ix

Contents

Executive Summary

INTRODUCTION

Widely used for sport and recreational purposes throughout the United States, black and smokeless powders in the retail market are sold primarily for reloading of ammunition and for use in muzzle-loading firearms, respectively. Large quantities of these powders are also used for military purposes. In addition, smokeless powder is used in ammunition manufactured for civilian use, and moderate amounts of black powder are used for blasting in the mining industry. Besides serving these legitimate purposes, black and smokeless powders can also be used to manufacture improvised explosive devices. Although bombs made from black or smokeless powder are usually small (particularly in comparison to the explosives used in incidents such as the World Trade Center and Oklahoma City bombings), they are the devices most commonly used in criminal bombings (FBI, 1997). Metal pipes are the containers used most often for effective black and smokeless powder bombs, which thus are frequently referred to as pipe bombs.

In response to events such as the 1995 Oklahoma City bombing, the U.S. Congress passed the Antiterrorism and Effective Death Penalty Act of 1996, which mandated a reexamination of the feasibility and desirability of adding markers and taggants to explosives.[1] The National Research Council (NRC)

---

[1] In this report, the term "marker" is used to describe any additive to black or smokeless powder designed to increase or assist in its detectability, with the particular goal of detecting a bomb before it explodes. The term "taggant" describes an additive with information content that could assist in the identification of the powder or its source. Initial studies of adding markers and taggants to explosives were summarized and analyzed in OTA (1980).

1

examined these issues for high explosives in its 1998 report *Containing the Threat from Illegal Bombings* (NRC, 1998). Black and smokeless powders were explicitly excluded from that study, but a 1997 amendment to the law required that the Treasury Department request a separate study of the technical feasibility of adding markers or taggants to black and smokeless powders. The NRC Committee on Smokeless and Black Powder responded by examining the relevant issues, with the goal of analyzing whether markers and taggants could be added to black and smokeless powders, while considering whether such additions would pose a risk to human life or safety; substantially assist law enforcement officers in their investigative efforts; substantially impair the quality and performance of the powders for their intended lawful use; have a substantial adverse effect on the environment; have costs that outweigh the benefits of their inclusion; and be susceptible to countermeasures.[2]

From 1979 to 1992 in the United States, the number of reported bombings involving black and smokeless powders approximately doubled (Hoover, 1995). However, between 1992 and 1996 (the most recent year for which data were available to the committee), the number of reported bombings involving these powders leveled off, averaging about 650 per year. From 1992 to 1994 the number of "significant" bombing incidents—defined by the committee as those that resulted in (or, for attempted bombings, had the capability of causing) death or injury or a minimum of $1,000 in property damage—was in the range of 250 to 300 per year.

Two federal agencies gather statistics on bombing incidents in the United States: the Department of the Treasury's Bureau of Alcohol, Tobacco, and Firearms (ATF) and the Department of Justice's Federal Bureau of Investigation (FBI). Each agency maintains separate statistics on bombing incidents, and each distributes its own form for voluntary reporting of incidents by local investigators. Discrepancies between the two data compilations complicate the analysis of the bombing threat.

DISCUSSION

Detection

Of all the approaches to reducing bombing incidents, detection of a bomb prior to explosion is the most attractive, since it provides an opportunity to render the bomb safe before it can cause death, injury, or property damage.

Three scenarios for the detection of bombs were considered by the committee: the *portal,* in which all people or packages entering an area must pass through a few well-monitored checkpoints (for example, at airports); the *suspicious pack-*

---

[2]See Appendix B for a complete statement of task.

age; and the *bomb threat,* in which there is reason to believe that there may be an explosive device somewhere within a large area, but its location is uncertain (as occurred in the Centennial Park bombing in Atlanta in July of 1996).

- *Portal scenario.* Because the powder containers in black and smokeless powder explosive devices must be thick enough to provide the substantial confinement of powder required to produce an effective explosion, they are likely to be visible on standard x-ray images. In addition, metal pipe bombs are readily detected by metal detectors, and dogs can detect a wide range of smokeless powders, black powders, and black powder substitutes and currently can be trained to detect devices containing any type of powder. However, dogs may quickly tire and are not well suited to the task of routine screening of large volumes of material.

- *Suspicious package scenario.* Portable standard x-ray systems currently used to examine suspicious packages can provide information about the type and location of an explosive device within the package that would assist in disarming the device. Vapor or residue detectors are becoming available that might be used to examine a suspicious package, but the results are likely to be less definitive. Dogs are known to be effective in examining suspicious packages.

- *Bomb threat scenario.* At present, searching by dogs or bomb squads is the only method for locating a bomb in a large area. Dogs combine high sensitivity to powders along with independent searching capability and thus enjoy a major advantage over other detection systems in this scenario. All other systems must be close to the device to function properly.

These three scenarios impose different requirements on detection systems. Portal systems are stationary, and so high capital cost may be tolerable if the system has a high throughput and low false alarm rate. In the suspicious package and bomb threat scenarios, system portability and low cost likely are more important. Despite progress in improving the detection of explosive materials with new technologies, current equipment can be expensive and is not always sufficiently sensitive or appropriately configured to detect all types of black or smokeless powder bombs.

The addition of markers to black or smokeless powder would be intended to enhance detection, particularly by low-cost, simple systems. An ideal marker would have the following characteristics: no real or perceived health or safety risks; wide applicability and utility for law enforcement; chemical and physical compatibility with black and smokeless powder; no adverse effect on powder or ballistic performance; no adverse environmental impact or contamination; low costs to various links in the chain of commerce; unique signature impossible to mask or contaminate; unique information that is easy to detect; and an appropriate lifetime.

Although 2,3-dimethyl-2,3-dinitrobutane (DMNB), one of the markers approved for use in plastic and sheet explosives under the International Civil Aviation Organization Convention, best meets the overall criteria for a suitable marker for high explosives, considering its incorporation into powders raises two potential concerns: DMNB is volatile and might evaporate during the typical shelf life of a black or smokeless powder sample; DMNB is also moderately toxic, and so its effects on those exposed to the marked product would have to be carefully assessed.[3]

The feasibility of detecting a bomb before it explodes depends on the target and the method of delivery. Most deaths and injuries caused by black powder or smokeless powder bombs have occurred in isolated, not public, surroundings,[4] and so these bombs were unlikely to have been detected through routine screening procedures. Although wider deployment of routine screening technologies is unlikely to affect significantly the number of victims of black and smokeless powder bombings, improving the capability of law enforcement personnel to deploy bomb detection technologies in response to an identified threat at a given site may still help to prevent casualties among bystanders and bomb squad personnel.

Identification

After a bombing takes place, information about improvised explosive devices must be obtained from material recovered at the scene. In bombing incidents in which black or smokeless powder is employed, many items of physical evidence typically survive a bomb blast. These items may include unexploded powder, chemical products of the reaction, and parts of the device such as the container used to enclose the powder, the container used to transport or conceal the device, triggering or delay mechanisms, and adhesive tape. Identification of the nonexplosive bomb components and the type of black or smokeless powder used in a bombing may aid in the identification and eventual conviction of the bomber.

Identification taggants are coded materials that can be added to a product by the manufacturer to provide information that can be "read" by investigators at some later stage in the use of the product. If taggants are to be effective, they must substantially enhance the steps in the forensic examination and lead to the faster apprehension and more certain conviction of the perpetrators.

A bomb container filled with black or smokeless powder often ruptures before all of the energetic material is consumed. The result is that unreacted powder, as well as decomposition residues in the case of black powder, can be

---

[3]The toxicity of DMNB is of less concern in its application to plastic and sheet explosives, because its toxicity is comparable to that of RDX, the main ingredient of these explosives (NRC, 1998).

[4]See Table 1.4 in Chapter 1 for more information on black and smokeless powder bombings by target.

recovered at the bomb scene and used in a forensic investigation. Both the FBI Explosives and Chemistry Units Laboratory and the National Laboratory Center of the ATF accumulate data on the physical dimensions and chemical composition of different types of smokeless powders, and they also keep samples and/or information about the physical dimensions of various commercially available black powders. However, in the course of criminal investigations, both laboratories have encountered black and smokeless powder samples that they are unable to identify based on their databases and samples.

Taggants could be used to facilitate the identification of the manufacturer and product line of black or smokeless powder used in a bomb without additional record keeping on the part of manufacturers or retailers. For example, the dyed powder added to some smokeless powders allows the user to immediately identify the specific product. However, it would be necessary to establish an audit trail to trace a particular powder used in a bomb from the manufacturer to the final purchaser. At each stage in the distribution system, sellers would have to record which tagged powders were sent to which customers, and retail outlets would have to keep their sales records in a form that could be readily accessed by investigators. Currently, record keeping generally ends when powder is shipped from the manufacturing facility to either distributors or retailers.

Establishing the characteristics of an ideal taggant for black and smokeless powders is the first step in assessing the practicality of real identification taggants. Ideal characteristics are by their nature unattainable, but by establishing these criteria, proposed taggant concepts may be judged against agreed-upon characteristics. The ideal taggant would have the following characteristics, which are not necessarily of equal importance: no real or perceived health or safety risks, forensic applicability and utility for law enforcement, chemical and physical compatibility with black and smokeless powders, no adverse effect on powder or ballistic performance, no adverse environmental impact or contamination, low cost to various links in the chain of commerce, no viable countermeasures, and unique information that is easy to read.

A large number of companies and other organizations proposed taggant concepts that were considered by this committee. One of these taggants has been used since 1980 in explosives in Switzerland, but many of the taggant technologies presented to the committee remain in the conceptual stage, and extensive research, development, and testing would be required to produce a viable commercial product.

Although not intended as such, some commercial smokeless powders in the United States do already incorporate a kind of taggant. These smokeless powders contain colored propellant granules that aid the reloader by providing a means for visual identification of the product. However, these dyed products also have served another purpose: bomb investigators have indicated to the committee that when the dyed powder granules are recovered at a bomb scene, they facilitate the identification of the powder used and aid the investigation.

Depending on the amount of information encoded in the taggant, the frequency with which the manufacturer changes the codes, and the extent of record keeping in the distribution system, tagging of black and smokeless powders could provide investigators with information on the manufacturer, specific product type, and chain of ownership. Taggants could also help to determine if different bombing incidents are connected, and once a suspect has been identified, taggants from a bomb scene could be matched with taggants found in the suspect's possession.

FINDINGS AND RECOMMENDATIONS

Information and Statistics

Finding: *Bombs that use black or smokeless powder cause a relatively small number of deaths and injuries, but their potential for use in terrorist activity is important.* Typically over the past 5 years, about 300 "significant"[5] bombing incidents each year have involved black or smokeless powder, and these bombings caused on the order of 10 deaths, 100 injuries, and $1 million in property damage annually.[6] Although the number of incidents attributable to terrorism is currently very low—in the range of one or two incidents per year—the committee notes that when bombing incidents are acts of terrorism, the target is larger than the physical location of the explosion, since a goal is to induce panic or fear among the general population.

Finding: *The databases on bombing statistics as currently compiled by two federal agencies contain serious discrepancies and are not sufficiently comprehensive.* To reach informed, appropriate decisions about legislation involving marking or tagging of explosives, policymakers need access to accurate and detailed information about the use and effects of improvised explosive devices in the United States. Improved data are needed so that interpretive correlations and trends in criminal activity can be readily extracted, especially for bombings judged to be "significant" according to specified criteria.

RECOMMENDED ACTION: A single, national database on bombing statistics that is comprehensive, searchable, and up-to-date should be established.

---

[5]Significant bombings represent actual bombings that caused at least one death, one injury, or a minimum of $1,000 in property damage, or attempted bombings aimed at targets where there was a potential for deaths, injuries, or major damage.

[6]Approximately 6 of those killed and 24 of those injured each year are perpetrators, people who are believed to have been involved in the construction or delivery of the explosive device.

Both the ATF and the FBI are currently improving their systems for handling the reporting, updating, and storage of bombing data in ways that should make the data more accessible and searchable for analysts. Incentives designed to encourage reporting of bombing incidents by local law enforcement agencies would increase the accuracy of federal data. A single reporting form submitted to a single database would reduce delays in publishing these data.

Detection

Finding: *Pipe bombs and similar explosive devices that use black and smokeless powders can be detected by exploiting both the properties of the powder itself and those of the container.*

Finding: *Current x-ray systems are capable of detecting explosive devices containing black and smokeless powders and are effective when placed at a portal or when used in portable equipment to examine a suspicious package. Current x-ray technologies are not suitable for quickly screening large numbers of packages or for performing large-area searches.* In addition, x-ray images must be examined by trained personnel or require the use of complex pattern recognition software to determine if the contents of a package resemble an explosive device.

Finding: *Both black and smokeless powders contain volatile compounds that are detectable by dogs. Canine searches are now the only viable means of conducting large-area searches for hidden explosive devices.* However, the circumstances that can interfere with canine detection of powders and the exact chemicals and concentrations of chemicals that dogs are able to detect are not currently well understood.

RECOMMENDED ACTION: Further research should be conducted on canine detection of bombs made with black and smokeless powders enclosed in various containers. Research should also be conducted on the development of inexpensive and portable instrumental sensors that mimic canine detection.

Better knowledge of how dogs detect devices containing black and smokeless powders would enable more efficient and appropriate use of dogs in examining large areas and buildings and would assist in the development of instruments capable of mimicking the methods by which dogs detect powders. Depending on their size, cost, and speed, such instruments could be used for large-area searches and for high-throughput, routine screening of packages.

Finding: *Detection markers added to black and smokeless powders could assist in the detection of explosive devices in several situations: large-area searches, examination of suspicious packages, rapid and routine screening of large numbers of packages, and enhancement of canine ability to detect black and smokeless powder bombs.* A detection marker's value to law enforcement for detecting explosive devices containing black and smokeless powder would depend on the properties of the added marker, such as its degree of detectability through a sealed pipe or layers of wrapping, and on the portability and cost of the associated detection equipment, as well as its range and sensitivity.

Finding: *No current marking system has been demonstrated to be technically feasible for use in black and smokeless powders.* While vapor markers have been successfully introduced into plastic and sheet explosives, there has not been a definitive study of how such markers might work in black and smokeless powders. Some issues of concern include the high volatility and the toxicity of vapor markers such as DMNB.

RECOMMENDATION: Detection markers in black and smokeless powders should not be implemented at the present time.

X-ray systems and dogs currently provide a strong capability for detecting bomb containers and unmarked black and smokeless powders in the scenarios considered by the committee, and most powder bombings currently take place at locations in which deployment of bomb detection systems is not practicable (see Table 1.4 in chapter 1). Therefore, the committee believes that the effectiveness of a marking program would be limited at the present time. Institution of a marking program would incur significant costs. At the current level of fewer than 10 deaths and 100 injuries per year and very few terrorist incidents, the committee believes that the benefits are not sufficient to justify such a marking program. If the threat were to increase substantially in the future and test data were available, benefits might exceed costs, and a marking program might be warranted. A marking program for black and smokeless powders would be justified only if three criteria were met: the frequency and severity of black and smokeless powder bombs were found to be high enough to justify marking; the markers first were thoroughly tested and found to be safe and effective under conditions likely to be encountered in the legal and illegal uses of the powders; and the social benefits of markers were found to outweigh the costs of their use.

RECOMMENDED ACTION: Research should be conducted to develop and test markers that would be technically suitable for inclusion in black and smokeless powders. The marking schemes studied should be those that would assist in large-area searches or rapid screening of a large number of packages.

More information and work are needed on marking technologies. Should it become necessary for policymakers to mandate the implementation of more intensive control procedures, the agencies concerned would then have the data necessary to make informed decisions about markers.

Identification

Finding: *More than 90 percent of the deaths and 80 percent of the injuries caused by pipe bombs that use black and smokeless powders occur in locations where security screening is not typically present.*[7] The lack of a viable detection system to screen for or locate explosive devices in these areas underscores the need for technologies that can assist law enforcement personnel in effectively investigating bombing incidents and prosecuting the offenders.

Finding: *The evidence that forensic investigators often recover at a bomb scene— such as unburned powder from smokeless powder bombs and characteristic residues or unburned powder from black powder devices—can enable identification of the powder manufacturer and product line, thereby assisting in investigation and prosecution.*

Finding: *The existing databases of information about black and smokeless powders, although used extensively in bombing investigations, are incomplete.* As of early 1998, the powder databases contained information on a significant fraction of the powders commercially available in the United States, but no systematic approach has been taken to developing a comprehensive powder database or to maintaining and updating the current information. In investigations forensic scientists do encounter black and smokeless powder samples that cannot be matched to samples in their powder databases.

RECOMMENDED ACTION: A comprehensive national powder database containing information about the physical characteristics and chemical composition of commercially available black and smokeless powders should be developed and maintained. Such a database would assist investigators in identifying the manufacturer and product line of these powders used in improvised explosive devices.

The ATF and the FBI share information contained in their powder databases. A joint database could provide a more efficient and effective tool for law enforcement.[8] Such an effort would also be strengthened by a formal program of coop-

---

[7]See Table 1.4 in Chapter 1 for more information on black and smokeless powder bombings by target.

[8]In addition, access to an easily searchable, comprehensive database could provide valuable assistance to state and local forensic investigators.

eration with the powder manufacturers to systematically collect product samples and gather official information about chemical composition and analytic protocols. An informal relationship already exists between the manufacturers and the forensic community in which the manufacturers' assistance is readily obtained during investigations of specific samples.

Finding: The minimal record keeping currently associated with the sale and distribution of black and smokeless powders does not allow tracing of a specific lot of powder from the manufacturer to the final retailer. At the retail level, there is no uniform, comprehensive system for keeping records of sales of powders; current practices vary from state to state, and there are relatively few locales in which any registration occurs.

Finding: Taggants added to black and smokeless powders and/or an associated record-keeping system could assist a bombing investigation by (1) aiding in the identification of the powder, manufacturer, and product line; (2) aiding in tracing the chain of ownership of the powder to a list of the last legal purchasers; and (3) helping to match the powder used in a bomb to powder in a suspect's possession. A taggant's usefulness would depend on the kinds and amount of coded information it contained; the strength of the audit trail would depend directly on that information and the nature of the system for recording sales. Use of a taggant would require decisions about how much information would be encoded, how often the information would be updated or changed, and whether the taggant and record-keeping costs would outweigh potential benefits.

Finding: No tagging system has been fully tested to demonstrate its technical feasibility for use in all types of black and smokeless powders, although in some cases taggants have been added to powders for specific applications. The use of taggants in Switzerland for black powders intended for blasting, and the use of dyed powder grains in some smokeless powder products in the United States, indicate that some forms of taggants are technically feasible for some powder products. However, the suspension of federally funded research on taggants in explosives applications in the United States in 1981 has left many questions unanswered about the compatibility of taggants with the wide variety of black and smokeless powder products currently available.[9] Although new taggant

---

[9]The Treasury, Postal Service and General Government Appropriation Bill, 1981 (Committee on Appropriations), Title I, p. 9: "After considering all the factors involved, particularly a Congressional Office of Technology Assessment report, the [House Committee on Appropriations] is concerned that the state of the art in explosives tagging technology is not sufficiently advanced to warrant either implementation or further research and development of this particular program at this time." The committee is not aware of any federally funded research on taggants in explosive materials that has occurred since this appropriations report.

concepts have been proposed that may overcome some of the safety and compatibility concerns raised by the 3M-type taggant currently used in Switzerland, thorough studies have not been performed on the use of any of these proposed taggants in black and smokeless powders.

RECOMMENDATION: Identification taggants in black and smokeless powder should not be implemented at the present time.

Institution of a taggant program with its associated record-keeping system would incur significant costs. At the current threat level of fewer than 10 deaths and 100 injuries per year and very few terrorist incidents, the committee believes that benefits are not sufficient to justify a tagging program. If the threat increased substantially in the future and test data were available, benefits might exceed costs, and a tagging program might be warranted.

A taggant program for black and smokeless powders would be justified only if three criteria were met: the frequency and severity of black and smokeless powder bombings were found to be high enough to justify tagging, the taggants first were thoroughly tested and found to be safe and effective under conditions likely to be encountered in the legal and illegal uses of the powders, and the benefits to society of taggants were found to outweigh the costs of their use. Since no tagging system has been fully tested to demonstrate its technical feasibility, it is not practicable to tag at this time.

RECOMMENDED ACTION: Research should be conducted to develop and test taggants that would be technically suitable for inclusion in black and smokeless powders should future circumstances warrant their use.

Although the committee believes that the current level of bombings using black and smokeless powders does not warrant the use of taggant technology, the situation could change for the worse in the future. If policymakers decide that the level and type of bombings require action to increase the tools available to help the investigators of bombing incidents, more needs to be known about what technologies would be helpful. Research needs to focus on discovering and testing taggant concepts in the context of the ideal taggant criteria described by the committee in Chapter 3 and in the context of the capabilities of the forensic community to identify untagged powders.

RECOMMENDATION: If the type or number of bombing incidents involving black and smokeless powders increases in a way that leads policymakers to believe that current investigatory and prosecutorial capabilities must be supplemented, the committee recommends that use of taggants, additional record keeping, or a combination of both actions be considered, provided that the chosen taggant technology has satisfactorily met all of the appropri-

ate technological criteria. Research on taggants, as recommended above, is therefore essential to develop options and demonstrate the technical viability of any taggant system that may be considered for implementation at a future date.

The response to an increased bombing threat would depend on the nature of these bombings and the state of the technologies available when the decisions are being made. The type of taggant program and/or level of record keeping could be chosen to reflect the threat that these measures are meant to counteract. Any tagging or record-keeping action considered would have to be evaluated in light of the costs and benefits associated with that particular option.

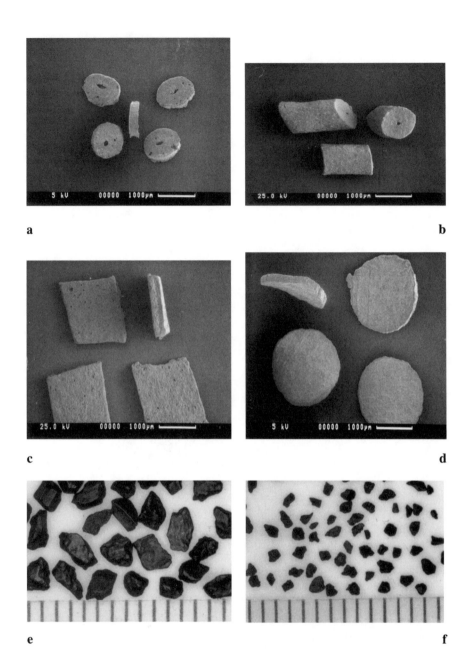

Black and smokeless powders. (a) "perforated disc" smokeless powder. (b) "tube" smokeless powder. (c) "cut square" smokeless powder. (d) "disc" smokeless powder. (e) Grade Fg black powder. (f) Grade FFFg (3Fg) black powder. Photographs a-d courtesy of the Federal Bureau of Investigation Chemistry Unit's powder morphology database. Photographs e and f courtesy of Rho Sigma Associates, Inc.

1

Background and Overview

INTRODUCTION

Black and smokeless powders are widely available for purchase throughout the United States in sporting stores and gun clubs. Some 3.5 million individuals purchase these powders each year for sport use.[1] These individuals include hunters and target shooters who prefer to hand load their own ammunition, as well as those who operate muzzle-loading weapons in reenactments and for hunting. Black powder is also used in the lift charges of fireworks, both for use in large-scale public displays and in fireworks sold for personal use.

In the hands of criminals, however, black and smokeless powders can be used to fill a variety of containers (e.g., pipes, tubes, or bottles) to make very effective bombs. Although these powder devices are not well suited for use in large-scale bombings, such as those that occurred at New York City's World Trade Center in 1993 or Oklahoma City's Murrah Federal Building in 1995, they were used in several recent terrorist incidents, including the Centennial Park bombing at the Olympics in Atlanta in 1996 and in several devices mailed by the Unabomber.[2] According to the Department of the Treasury's Bureau of Alcohol,

---

[1]Statement of the Sporting Arms and Ammunition Manufacturers' Institute in the H.R. 1710 (The Comprehensive Anti-Terrorism Act of 1995) hearings before the House Committee on the Judiciary, June 13, 1995, distributed to the committee on January 15, 1998.

[2]According to information provided to the committee by the FBI, the first seven bombings committed by the Unabomber between 1978 and 1982 involved devices with commercial smokeless powder as the filler. In subsequent devices, the Unabomber used improvised mixtures of chemicals.

Tobacco, and Firearms (ATF) and the Department of Justice's Federal Bureau of Investigation (FBI), black and smokeless powders are the explosive materials most commonly used in improvised explosive devices in the United States; in 1995 these propellants were in roughly one-third of all such devices (ATF, 1997; FBI, 1997).

Markers and Taggants

Law enforcement agencies at the federal, state, and local levels invest substantial resources to address the bombing problem by detecting and disarming bombs before they go off, as well as by tracing the origins of explosives and other residual material found at a bomb scene. To facilitate these efforts, researchers in the 1970s investigated whether two types of substances added to explosives— markers and taggants—could enhance the capabilities of law enforcement agencies to detect devices before they explode, or to identify and prosecute those responsible (OTA, 1980). In this study, the term "markers" is used to describe any additive to smokeless or black powder designed to increase or assist in detectability. Markers could help in detecting an explosive material before the bomb can be activated and could assist crime scene investigators in determining where to look for evidence after an explosion. The term "taggants" is used to represent any material that can be added to smokeless or black powder in order to assist in identifying the powder or its sources. One type of taggant, a multilayered plastic chip, was tested extensively in explosives, including black and smokeless powders (OTA, 1980; Aerospace Corporation, 1980).[3] Support for this research was terminated in the United States in 1981,[4] leaving a number of questions unanswered, particularly concerning that taggant's compatibility with some explosive formulations, including smokeless powders. In the interim, however, the same taggant has been used without any reported problems in Switzerland for high explosives and black powder intended for blasting. Although there was no continuing work on taggants for explosive materials in the United States, various taggant concepts have found application in the prevention of counterfeiting and in quality control of commercial products ranging from gasoline to perfumes.[5]

---

[3]This type of taggant, a multilayered plastic chip, was developed by Richard Livesay in the 1970s and licensed to the Minnesota Mining and Manufacturing (3M) Company. Currently, this technology is used by Microtrace, Inc.

[4]The Treasury, Postal Service and General Government Appropriation Bill, 1981 (Committee on Appropriations), Title I, p. 9.

[5]Some commercial applications of taggants for prevention of counterfeiting and for product identification are given in Schlesinger (1998). Also see descriptions of individual taggant concepts in Appendix D for more information on nonexplosive applications for taggants.

Origin and Scope of This Study

Responding to increased concerns about terrorism, including the bombing of the Murrah Federal Building in Oklahoma City in 1995, Congress passed the Antiterrorism and Effective Death Penalty Act of 1996. In this act, Congress mandated a reexamination of the feasibility and desirability of adding markers and taggants to explosives. The National Research Council (NRC) examined these issues for high explosives in a 1998 report, *Containing the Threat from Illegal Bombings* (NRC, 1998); however, black and smokeless powders were explicitly excluded from the scope of that report, and the NRC was mandated to conduct a separate study of these powders (see Appendix B). The Committee on Smokeless and Black Powder responded to that mandate.

This report of the committee focuses on the detection of devices containing smokeless and black powders and the capability to identify the perpetrator of a bombing from powders recovered at a bomb scene. Two questions are relevant: the first concerns the technical feasibility of adding markers or taggants to a smokeless or black powder; the second and more involved question is whether the economic and social benefits of the addition of markers or taggants outweigh the economic and social costs. The Act stipulates that the study examine the inclusion of markers or taggants in smokeless and black powder in light of several issues: safety, assistance to law enforcement officers' investigative efforts, effect on powder performance in lawful uses, environmental impact, costs to manufacturers and consumers, and susceptibility to countermeasures.[6] In the discussion of record keeping that supplements Chapter 3's discussion of taggants for black or smokeless powders, the committee focuses on the retail sale of canister powders to the public for reloading and muzzle loading. Detailed examination of the distribution and tracking systems for the products that use these powders (such as ammunition and fireworks, or pyrotechnics) was not included in this study, because currently the easiest, cheapest, and most common method of obtaining black or smokeless powder for use in a bomb is to purchase the powder that is available in canisters.

For several reasons beyond the explicit wording in the charge to the committee (see Appendix B), pyrotechnic compositions are not examined in this study. A broad range of chemical compositions with a large variety of uses can be classified as pyrotechnics, and the systems for manufacturing and distributing them are diverse. Moreover, many pyrotechnic substances can be produced by mixing readily available precursor chemicals.[7]

---

[6]See Appendix B for a description of the enabling legislation and the statement of task.

[7]The issues related to controls on precursor chemicals were discussed in a recent NRC report (NRC, 1998).

Although pyrotechnics are reported as the explosive material in many bombing incidents, most of these have involved devices that used cardboard containers,[8] suggesting that fireworks are being purchased and used without alteration for illegal purposes. If legislation mandating the marking or tagging of black powder were to be enacted, the uses of pyrotechnic compositions and of black powder in fireworks as potential countermeasures to the effectiveness of such laws would have to be considered. A brief description of pyrotechnic compositions and devices is given in Box 1.1.

BLACK AND SMOKELESS POWDERS: CHARACTERISTICS, PRODUCTION, AND DISTRIBUTION

Any discussion of marking or tagging black or smokeless powders must be informed by an understanding of the variety of legal uses for these powders, the manufacturing processes that produce these powders, and the distribution and sales systems that bring the powders to users.

Chemical Composition, Properties, and Legal Uses

Literally hundreds of different black and smokeless powder products are produced by a number of processes. The exact compositions of the products are tailored to produce very specific performance characteristics. However, products nominally designed for the same uses but made by different manufacturers may have been formulated quite differently to meet the same performance specifications. This section provides more detail on the nature of black and smokeless powders (including chemical composition and morphology) and some of the common uses for these powders. This background is necessary for the discussion in Chapter 3 on the use of powders as physical evidence in bombing investigations.

Black Powders and Black Powder Substitutes

The oldest propellant is black powder. Numerous historical works trace the invention of this powder to the Chinese several millennia ago. From China, the technology spread to Central Asia and was brought to Europe by the Arabs about the middle of the 13th century. During their siege of Niebla in Spain in 1257, missiles that probably contained a composition resembling black powder were used. Later accounts show black powder being used as an industrial or mining explosive as early as the 16th century (Urbanski, 1967; Cooper and Kurowski, 1996; Davis, 1943; Ball, 1961; Taylor, 1959).

---

[8]Unpublished data received from the ATF for the years 1992 to 1994 indicate that, of those incident reports listing containers, 61 percent of bombs involving pyrotechnics were in cardboard.

BOX 1.1 Pyrotechnic Compositions and Devices

The term "pyrotechnics" is used to describe particular chemical compositions and devices and the effects that they can produce, such as heat, light, smoke, gas, sound, and motion. Pyrotechnic compositions normally consist of one or more oxidizers combined with one or more fuels, binders, or other additives. Pyrotechnic devices are manufactured in many shapes and sizes to meet specific needs and can contain pyrotechnic compositions in amounts ranging from as little as a few milligrams to as much as tens of pounds. Black powder is also employed in many pyrotechnic devices but is not present in all such devices. It is most commonly used in fuses and as a propelling or bursting charge.

Pyrotechnic devices can be divided into two classes: civilian and military. Typically it is the intended use of the device that determines its class, not the chemistry of the pyrotechnic composition. Military pyrotechnics include signal and countermeasure flares, signal and obscuration smokes, tracer compositions, incendiaries, and igniters. Civilian pyrotechnics include matches, signaling devices such as highway flares and railroad fusees, automotive air-bag inflators, toy caps, model rocket motors, theatrical special effects, and fireworks.

Fireworks often include black powder as well as pyrotechnic compositions.[1] The amount of black powder used ranges from a fraction of an ounce in consumer, off-the-shelf fireworks to several pounds in aerial display devices.[2] Compared to purchasing a 1- or 2-pound canister of black powder, obtaining an equivalent amount of powder by purchasing fireworks and extracting the black powder would be more difficult, more time consuming, more dangerous, and considerably more expensive.

The shelf life of pyrotechnic devices varies, depending on the type of device and the conditions under which it is stored. As is the case for black powder, moisture can cause deterioration.

---

[1]Black powder substitutes are used only occasionally in fireworks, and smokeless powders are not used at all.

[2]Access to display fireworks is very restricted. Manufacturers and distributors must be licensed, and display fireworks can be sold legally only to end users who have permits issued by local authorities. Display fireworks are normally stored long term in ATF-inspected magazines, and they are handled administratively as explosives, with the associated record keeping.

Black powder consists of a combination of the fuels charcoal and sulfur along with the oxidizing agent potassium nitrate.[9] No chemical reactions are involved in the manufacturing process, which depends entirely on the intimate physical mixing of the ingredients in fixed proportions. The physical properties

---

[9]Some black powders, designated as "Grade B blasting," use sodium nitrate instead of potassium nitrate. Military grades JAN A, B, and C also use sodium nitrate.

and performance characteristics of black powder are strongly dependent on the method of manufacture (the equipment used and the process parameters) and the purity of the ingredients. Black powder substitutes are also available commercially as a replacement for black powder in some applications. These powders are formulated using one or more oxidizers, such as potassium nitrate and potassium perchlorate, in combination with fuels such as sulfur, charcoal, ascorbic acid, sodium benzoate, starches, and sugars.

Black powder is currently used as a propellant and an explosive in a variety of applications. It is used in muzzle-loading weapons for hunting or in historical reenactments. It is also employed as the propellant for motors in small model rockets and is the powder core in safety fuses. Fireworks manufacturers use black powder extensively, for example in timing fuses and in lift charges for aerial display devices. Mining companies use black powder as an explosive for blasting. The military uses black powder in small rockets, delay trains, and mine projectors, and in gun-propellant primers and igniters. In some of these applications, black powder substitutes can be used in place of genuine black powder. For example, the substitutes now are used often in muzzle-loading weapons, but they have limited applications in fireworks.

Black powder and its substitutes can remain viable indefinitely, retaining their properties if the powders are properly packaged and/or stored to exclude moisture.

Smokeless Powders

In the 20th century, smokeless powders have largely replaced black powder in handguns, rifles, and larger-caliber weapons. Smokeless powders are not truly smokeless but, in comparison to black powder, the "smoke" products produced when smokeless powders are used in ammunition are much cleaner. Smokeless powders are generally grouped in three broad categories, based on their chemical compositions: single base, double base, and triple base. The first two categories are commonly used and commercially available; the last type, like the more chemically complex composite propellants, is for specialty applications and is not sold to the general public.

Single-base propellants contain nitrocellulose (NC) as the energetic material.[10] Various stabilizers are blended with the NC to reduce degradation of the powder over time. Propellant granules may also be coated with burning-rate modifiers, flash suppressants, or deterrents in order to control performance characteristics. The powder is also glazed with graphite to reduce sensitivity to ignition by static electricity and to improve flow characteristics.

---

[10]The nitrocellulose used in single-based smokeless powders has a nitrogen content between 12.6 percent and 13.3 percent.

Double-base propellants are also made with NC but are plasticized with another explosive or energetic material that is often a liquid, usually nitroglycerin (NG). This second component, which may be up to 40 percent of the total by mass, is used to adjust the oxygen balance. This plasticizer, along with other additives, can be used to optimize performance parameters such as burn rate and reaction temperature. As with single-base propellants, stabilizers are added to increase shelf life and granules are coated to control performance. Some double-base powder granules are produced in various colors to help users distinguish between different types of powders, but most powder is glazed with graphite. For both single- and double-base powders, shelf lives of 20 to 30 years can reliably be expected. There have been examples of smokeless powders that have not been exposed to high temperatures proving serviceable even after 40 to 60 years.

Surface area per unit mass of the propellant is a key characteristic for determining the overall burn rate and hence performance. To achieve the intended performance, propellant granules are produced in a variety of shapes and sizes including disks, cut squares, tubes, and flattened balls, the dimensions of which are optimized to achieve predictable and repeatable performance.

Triple-base propellants add a third reactive material, nitroguanidine (NQ), to the NC and NG. By varying the percentage of each of the reactive ingredients and adding other ingredients, such as oxidizers, plasticizers, and stabilizers, compositions are formulated to achieve specified performance parameters. Triple-base propellants are used mainly by the military, typically in large-caliber guns. Another class of specially formulated propellants is composite propellants in which the oxidizers and fuels are separate materials.[11] These propellants are used in a variety of applications, including as rocket fuel and as gas generators.[12,13]

Triple-base powders and composite propellants are manufactured for specialty uses and not sold to the general public. Single- and double-base smokeless powders are produced mainly for use in ammunition and are sold to both ammunition manufacturers and sporting shooters for this purpose. People who buy smokeless powders in order to assemble and reload their own ammunition do so for a variety of reasons. The two strongest motivations are cost and performance. Purchasing the individual components of ammunition (the bullet, powder, car-

---

[11]Composite propellants typically do not include volatile ingredients, such as the nitrate esters found in conventional double-base smokeless powder, and therefore have very low vapor pressures. This characteristic makes these powders more difficult to detect with certain types of detection equipment; see Chapter 2.

[12]See summary of presentation by James Scheld, Indian Head Division, Naval Surface Warfare Center, in Appendix E.

[13]As triple-base powders and composite propellants are difficult to obtain currently, they are seldom used in improvised explosive devices. However, if the use of commercial powders in such devices were curtailed through regulations, marking, or tagging, then the specialty propellants might be viewed as a possible alternative explosive material for the makers of illegal devices.

tridge case, and initiator, for example) separately and reusing the cartridge cases can enable the reloader to realize savings of as much as 50 percent over store-bought ammunition. In addition, by hand loading ammunition, the shooter has much more control over the exact specifications of the ammunition and therefore over the performance (National Shooting Sports Foundation, 1996).[14]

Producers of Black and Smokeless Powders

Black and smokeless powders sold in the United States are manufactured by a small number of U.S. companies and imported from foreign companies all over the world. In addition to retail sales to consumers, these powders are sold to U.S. and foreign militaries, companies that manufacture ammunition, and other commercial firms, such as fireworks producers.

Black Powders and Black Powder Substitutes

Most of the black powder sold in the United States is manufactured domestically; a small amount is imported from Slovenia, Brazil, China, Germany, and Switzerland.[15] Commercial customers range from muzzle loaders who buy 1-pound canisters, to companies that manufacture fireworks, model rockets, or safety fuses, to mining concerns buying large quantities for blasting.[16] The U.S. military is also a major user. Some quantity of black powder is also imported into this country within premade fireworks, mainly from China.

Currently, the only major manufacturer of black powder in the United States is Goex, Inc., located at the Louisiana Army Ammunition Plant. However, black powder is also imported, both in individual canisters for direct sale to consumers and in bulk quantities for repackaging by U.S. companies. A wider variety of black powder substitutes are made in the United States, including Pyrodex from the Hodgdon Powder Company, Clean Shot Powder from Clean Shot Technologies, Inc., and Black Mag from the Arco Powder Company. While no U.S. companies have begun manufacturing black powder in the past half century, the number of black powder substitutes made and available in the United States is growing.

---

[14]Also, personal communication from Robert T. Delfay, president and chief executive officer, Sporting Arms and Ammunition Manufacturers' Institute, and Bill Chevalier, president, National Reloading Manufacturers' Association. See also Appendix F, which includes a report on the committee's site visit to the National Rifle Association headquarters, for more information.

[15]Personal communication from Mick Fahringer, Goex, Inc., July 22, 1998.

[16]According to Mick Fahringer, Goex, Inc., June 9, 1998, roughly 100,000 to 150,000 pounds of black-powder-type propellant are used in blasting applications per year.

Smokeless Powders

Approximately 10 million pounds of commercial smokeless powders are sold in the United States each year. Roughly 70 percent of this amount is sold to original equipment manufacturers (OEMs) to be put directly into ammunition. The remaining quantity is sold in individual canisters (ranging from 1/2-pound cans to 12- or 20-pound kegs) to reloaders for personal use. These purchases can occur in gun stores, retail outlets (such as Wal-Mart or K-Mart), or through hunting and shooting clubs. A large quantity of smokeless powder is also manufactured for sale to domestic and foreign militaries.

In North America, the major producers of smokeless powders are Alliant Techsystems (previously Hercules, Inc.) in Radford, Virginia; PRIMEX Technologies (previously Olin Corporation) in St. Marks, Florida; and Expro Chemical Products, Inc. (improved military rifle propellants previously manufactured by E.I. DuPont) in Valleyfield, Quebec, Canada. Numerous other companies import smokeless powders into the United States. These companies include Australia Defense Industries, Lovex (Czech Republic), Bofors (Sweden), Vihtavouri (Finland), and SNPE (France). Often these companies' products are repackaged by U.S. companies, such as Hodgdon Powder Company and Accurate Arms, for commercial sales within the United States.

Distribution Systems

Both black and smokeless powders are sold to individuals at a variety of retail outlets. The powder manufacturers and repackagers disburse their products to these businesses through a system of approximately 20 master distributors in North America. These companies buy large quantities of canister powders, which are then resold in smaller quantities to smaller distributors and wholesalers, who in turn supply cans to dealers, gun shops, shooting clubs, hardware stores, and other retailers. Consumers can purchase a 1-pound canister of black or smokeless powder for $15 to $20 at a standard retail outlet. The cost per pound can be lower if the quantity purchased is large (e.g., a 20-pound keg) or if the purchase is made through a gun club.

Currently, the powder manufacturers' systems are not designed to ensure that one blended lot of a particular type of powder goes to a single master distributor. In some cases, powders are packaged for retail sale at the manufacturing site and are sold by the manufacturers directly to the master distributors; at other times powder is sold in bulk by the manufacturers to other powder sellers and to original equipment manufacturers, who repackage the powders and sell under their own labels.

Powders produced for military use can be distributed in several ways. They can be sold directly to the U.S. military for various uses. They can be loaded into ammunition by the powder manufacturer, and the ammunition then sold to military users. The powders can be shipped to military subcontractors for loading into ammunition. Finally, they can be exported for sale to friendly foreign governments and foreign loading companies. Military surplus powders are sometimes sold back to powder manufacturers for reuse as raw materials or to repackagers for sale in the commercial market.[17]

Figure 1.1 outlines the various paths smokeless and black powders take from manufacturers to users.

Manufacturing Processes

In gathering information for this study, the committee heard presentations from industry organizations and individual companies (see Appendix E). In addition, subgroups of the committee made several site visits to various plants to observe the manufacturing process and equipment used in producing and packaging smokeless and black powders (see Appendix F). The following descriptions are brief summaries of the manufacturing practices in use in the industry today. This background is necessary for the discussion in Chapters 2 and 3 on the feasibility and desirability of adding markers or taggants to these powders.

Black Powders and Black Powder Substitutes

The performance of black powder depends in large part on the process by which it is manufactured. Over the decades, certain equipment and procedures have been found to yield powder with desirable characteristics, and these methods have become the standard for black powder manufacture. Today, black powder is produced by combining the three main ingredients (sulfur, charcoal, and potassium nitrate) in heavy wheel mills that mix and crush the powder.[18] The tremendous pressures in the mill cause the sulfur to plasticize and flow, thereby binding the charcoal and nitrate. The mixture is then pressed into blocks and passed through a series of rollers to break the chunks into granules of various sizes. Vibrating screens are then used to separate the granules into consistently sized batches. This screening produces the various grades of black powder, as the bulk burning rate is a function of particle size. Finally, the granules are coated with graphite before being sifted, weighed, and packaged. While the composition and morphologies of black powder substitutes differ from those of genuine black powder, the manufacturing process is fairly similar.

---

[17]If a powder marking or tagging program were to be instituted, the contributions of these surplus military powders to the commercial market would have to be considered and accounted for.

[18]The typical composition is approximately 75 percent potassium nitrate, 15 percent charcoal, and 10 percent sulfur.

25

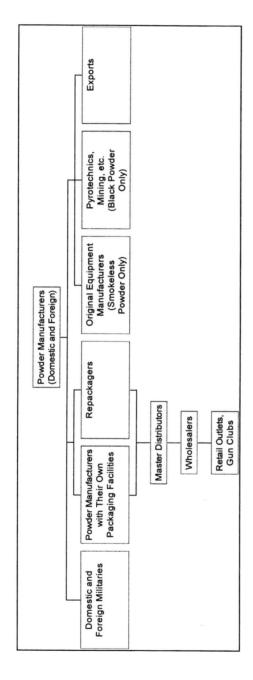

FIGURE 1.1 Distribution system for smokeless and black powders. This diagram represents the most common distribution chains for black and smokeless powders, although there are exceptions in some cases. For example, some repackagers ship directly to retail outlets, and some small original equipment manufacturers purchase smokeless powder from master distributors.

SOURCE: Presentations from and site visits to Goex, Inc., Alliant Techsystems, PRIMEX Technologies, Hodgdon Powder Company, and Winchester Ammunition.

Smokeless Powders

As described above, the three categories of chemical composition for smokeless powders are single base, double base, and triple base. Also, two distinct types of manufacturing processes result in two different morphologies: smokeless extruded powders and smokeless ball powders. This section briefly describes the two processes used to produce double-base propellant, the most common of the commercially available smokeless powders.

At the beginning of the extruded smokeless powder process, the major ingredients are mixed together with solvents to form a dough. In double-base powders, these ingredients are NC and NG. Some minor ingredients, such as flash suppressants, stabilizers, opacifiers, and dyes, may also be added at this stage. The relative percentages of the different components are varied to produce the performance characteristics desired for the final product. The mixture is then pressed into blocks that can be fed into the extrusion press and cutting machine. The extrusion press forces the doughlike mixture through precision metal dies, and the strands are cut by a spinning knife to produce grains of various diameters and shapes, depending on the extrusion and cutting parameters. Perforations in the granules can also be added at this stage. The resultant powder granules can be long thin cylinders or flat flakes or a variety of other geometries. The shape and the surface area per unit mass of the granules contribute to the burn rate and other characteristics that affect performance. The granules are then screened to ensure that the size of the granules in a given lot is consistent. Next, the solvents are extracted, and various coatings, such as deterrents and graphite, are applied to the surface of the granules. The powder is then dried and screened again. At this point, the powder is blended to ensure homogeneity, and samples are taken to test the ballistic performance of the propellant. This quality control is done by hand loading the powder into the type of ammunition for which it has been developed and testing the performance of the ammunition. Adjustments can be made by blending different batches to obtain the desired performance.

When smokeless ball powder is being made, the initial mix of ingredients includes only NC, stabilizers, and solvents. These components are blended into a dough, extruded through a pelletizing plate, and precipitated into spheres. The solvent is then removed, and the granules are screened to produce groups with narrow size distributions. NG is then impregnated into the granules, and the surfaces are coated with deterrents. Next, rollers are used to flatten the spherical granules; by varying the surface area of the granules, the manufacturers can gain further control over performance characteristics such as burn rate. Additional coating with graphite and flash suppressants occurs at the next step. After another screening stage, the batch is mixed to ensure homogeneity, and samples are taken to test the ballistic performance of the propellant. As with extruded smokeless powder, blending of batches often occurs to ensure that performance standards are met.

General Comments on the Manufacturing Processes

All the processes described above have some characteristics in common that are relevant to issues related to marking or tagging of black or smokeless powders. While some elements of these processes may be continuous, propellants, on the whole, are manufactured in batches or lots.[19] In general, a good deal of recycling of materials occurs; unsatisfactory material may be removed from a given batch and returned to the beginning or near the beginning of the process for use in another lot. Such material may be rejected owing to a variety of factors, such as granules that are too small or too large, or poor performance in quality control tests. Not only can partially processed powder be recycled, but the manufacturers also reuse finished products. Such material may come from returns by the distributors or from surplus or obsolete military powders purchased cheaply to be used as a low-cost source of raw materials. All of this reworking and recycling in the manufacturing process serves three purposes: (1) to assure good quality control of the final product, (2) to reduce costs by reusing material that fails to meet performance specifications, and (3) to reduce pollution by avoiding destruction of such material by burning (the only legal way to destroy a discarded propellant). The issue of reworked powders, with the attendant mixing of powders with varying origins, would be an important consideration in the possible implementation of a marker or taggant scheme.

BLACK AND SMOKELESS POWDERS IN IMPROVISED EXPLOSIVE DEVICES

The construction of an effective bomb using black or smokeless powder requires several components, including, at a minimum, a robust container, the propellant powder, and an initiation system (for a rough sketch, see Figure 3.1 in Chapter 3). Other common potential elements include a power source, a timing device, and nails or tacks. As discussed in Chapters 2 and 3, the nonpowder components in the device may play an important role in detecting the bomb or identifying the perpetrator.

The typical black or smokeless powder pipe bomb contains approximately 1/2 pound of powder and is roughly 10 inches long and 1 inch wide.[20] This is a relatively small device when compared to the truck bombs used at the Murrah Federal Building and the World Trade Center. In general, bombs that use black and smokeless powders tend to be "package size" rather than "car size" for two reasons: cost and containment. Using approximate values, powders are $15 per pound, while dynamite is $1.50 per pound, and the explosive mixture of ammo-

---

[19]The typical lot is between 10,000 and 20,000 pounds, with a range of 5,000 pounds (for specialty powders) to 50,000 pounds (for military ammunition), according to written materials received from the Sporting Arms and Ammunition Manufacturers' Institute by the committee on January 15, 1998.

[20]Presentation to the committee by Roger Broadbent, Virginia State Police, January 15, 1998.

nium nitrate and fuel oil (ANFO) is $0.15 per pound. Therefore, for very large explosive devices, use of powder is not cost-effective. In addition, powders require containment to produce an explosion, and it is difficult to buy, construct, or safely transport a container sufficiently robust to be used in a very large powder bomb. These two factors explain why large-scale powder bombs are not used. However, the issues related to cost and containment are less problematic on a small scale, and are compensated for by the fact that small quantities of powder currently are much easier to obtain than dynamite or ANFO and that, unlike these explosives, powders can be initiated by flame.

Metal pipes are the most common containers used for effective black and smokeless powder bombs, while cardboard tubes are the most common containers used for bombs filled with pyrotechnic powders.[21] However, many other types of containers have been used, including plastic pipe, cans, glass and plastic bottles, grenade hulls, and even tennis balls. The primary purpose of the containers is to confine the gases produced during the burning of the explosive powder. The resulting pressure then explodes the container. The fragments of the container are propelled outward at high speeds to cause deaths, injuries, and property damage. Nails or tacks taped to the outside of the container are designed to increase the number of dangerous fragments produced in the explosion. Often, the bomb itself is placed within a larger package, such as a box, a suitcase, or a knapsack (as in Centennial Park). The primary purposes of the packaging are usually ease of transport and concealment.

An initiation system is designed to start the black or smokeless powder burning within a pipe bomb. Simple examples of such systems include a cigarette with one end imbedded in the powder (Scott, 1994) or a match, a length of safety fuse, and a charge of black powder (Stoffel, 1972). More elaborate systems may include a complex timing apparatus or triggering devices that operate remotely or are designed to be set off by the intended victim (as in car bombs). The use of any particular mode of initiation will result in potentially useful physical evidence being recovered at the crime scene: lengths of safety fuse, wires, springs, percussion caps, fragments of batteries, fragments of clocks, and the like.

STATISTICS ON THE USE OF IMPROVISED EXPLOSIVE DEVICES CONTAINING BLACK AND SMOKELESS POWDERS

Two federal agencies gather statistics on bombing incidents in the United States: the ATF and the FBI.[22] This study relied on bombing statistics supplied by

---

[21]Cardboard containers were used in 61 percent of pyrotechnic bombing incidents in which the container was reported, and metal pipes were used for 62 percent of smokeless and black powder bombing incidents in which the container was reported, according to ATF data for 1992-1994.

[22]The U.S. Postal Inspection Service investigates and tracks bombs sent through the mail. The total number of such devices has averaged about 16 per year between 1983 and 1997. Unpublished materials received from the U.S. Postal Inspection Service.

both the ATF and the FBI. Each agency maintains a separate statistics database on bombing incidents, and each has its own form for use by local investigators who are reporting incidents.[23] No law requires local investigators to report a bombing incident to either the ATF or the FBI; both the initial reporting of an incident and any subsequent updating as the investigation proceeds are done on a voluntary basis. Although these agencies exchange information on bombing cases reported to them, and although they go through an annual data-reconciliation process intended to result in a common set of numbers, discrepancies nevertheless remain that complicated the committee's analysis of the bombing threat.[24] Previous attempts to analyze bombing statistics have met with similar problems (OTA, 1980; White House Commission, 1997; and NRC, 1998).

Total Number of Reported Bombings Involving Black and Smokeless Powders

Table 1.1 shows the number of actual and attempted bombings reported in the United States involving black and smokeless powders[25] in the 5-year period from 1992 to 1996. Over this period, the number of reported bombings using

---

[23]Public Law 104-208 specified that "the Secretary (of the Treasury) is authorized to establish a national repository of information on incidents involving arson and the suspected criminal misuse of explosives. All Federal agencies having information concerning such incidents shall report the information to the Secretary pursuant to such regulations as deemed necessary to carry out the provisions of this subsection. . . ." The Uniform Federal Crime Reporting Act of 1988 states that the "Attorney General may designate the Federal Bureau of Investigation as the lead agency" to "acquire, collect, classify, and preserve national data on Federal criminal offenses as part of the Uniform Crime Reports."

[24]For instance, the number of actual and attempted bombings involving black and smokeless powders in 1995 as reported by the ATF was 286 (ATF, 1997), while the FBI reported 624 (written materials from Gregory Carl, FBI). This difference was apparently caused by a change in the FBI reporting forms from 1994 to 1995, in which black and smokeless powder bombs, which were reported in separate categories in 1994, were combined in the same category in 1995. When the FBI reported the cases to the ATF using the new combined category, the ATF (which continues to keep the categories separate in its statistics database) could not definitively put the cases in either the black or smokeless powder category and chose not to enter those cases in any category.

Another example of discrepancies was apparent as a result of the committee's attempt to extract data on "significant" bombings—those actual bombings that caused at least one death, one injury, or $1,000 in property damage. Staff analysis of data provided by the ATF indicated that there were 160 such incidents in 1993 and 122 in 1994, while a computer search conducted by the FBI of its own statistics database found 80 such incidents in 1993 and 41 such incidents in 1994. The FBI suggested that one reason for the difference might be different estimates of property damage in the two statistics databases.

[25]To obtain a consistent data set over the 5-year period from 1992 through 1996, it was necessary to combine black and smokeless powder incidents into one category and to use data from different sources. Incidents involving black and smokeless powders were reported separately on FBI reports prior to 1995. For 1995, 1996, and 1997, incidents involving black and smokeless powders were combined on FBI reports. Starting in 1998, these categories will again be reported separately. Data from 1992 to 1994 are from the ATF. Data from 1995 and 1996 are from the FBI.

TABLE 1.1   All Reported Actual and Attempted Bombings Using Propellants, Pyrotechnics, and High Explosives Between 1992 and 1996

Type of Explosive Used	1992	1993[a]	1994	1995[b]	1996
Bomb containing smokeless powder/black powder/black powder substitutes					
Total incidents	667	637	696	624	643
Actual	524	498	447	454	405
Attempted	143	139	249	170	238
Deaths	9	12	6	8	13
Injuries	82	68	49	53	162
Property damage	$780K	$856K	$1.8M	$243K	$896K
Pyrotechnics/fireworks					
Total incidents	365	310	439	308	332
Actual	313	268	381	245	251
Attempted	52	42	58	63	81
Deaths	2	6	3	2	1
Injuries	126	54	87	33	36
Property damage	$171K	$253K	$237K	$122K	$95K
High explosives					
Total incidents	38	43	29	57	46
Actual	22	26	16	39	33
Attempted	16	17	13	18	13
Deaths	2	18	4	177	2
Injuries	3	1054	2	538	12
Property damage	$129K	$511M	$317K	$100M	$141K

NOTE: Actual or attempted bombings include incidents in which a device either exploded or was delivered to a target but did not explode. It does not include unexploded devices that were recovered by law enforcement personnel but not associated with a target.

[a]High-explosives data for 1993 include the figures from the World Trade Center bombing on February 26, 1993, in which 6 people were killed, 1,042 were injured, and $510 million of property damage was sustained.

[b]High-explosives data for 1995 include the anomalous carnage in the bombing of the Murrah Federal Building in Oklahoma City, in which 168 people were killed, 518 were injured, and roughly $100 million worth of property was damaged.

SOURCE: Adapted from unpublished data for 1992-1994 received from the ATF and for 1995-1996 from the FBI, and reports from the ATF (1997) and the FBI (1997).

black and smokeless powders remained relatively constant, averaging 653 per year. However, between 1979 and 1992, the number of bombings involving these powders approximately doubled (reflecting the general trend in bombings involving all types of explosives) (Hoover, 1995). Therefore, although the frequency of smokeless and black powder bombings does not appear to have increased significantly in recent years, it remains at a historically high level.[26]

---

[26]Because the statistics gathered by national agencies depend on state and local officials reporting bombing incidents to these agencies, it is not clear what percentage of the increase in bombings is due to a growth in the number of incidents and how much reflects improved reporting.

Table 1.1 also lists the deaths, injuries, and property damage attributable to the various types of devices from 1992 to 1996. The data show that bombs with black or smokeless powder fillers caused on the order of 10 deaths, 100 injuries, and $1 million in property damage in each of the 5 years.[27] For purposes of comparison, bombing incidents involving pyrotechnics and high explosives are also shown.

Analysis of the data for the years 1992-1994 shows that black and smokeless powders were used with roughly equal frequency.[28] During this period, there was an average of 364 incidents per year involving black powder and 302 per year involving smokeless powder.

"Significant" Reported Bombings

The data in Table 1.1 represent a mix of serious incidents that caused death and injury, as well as less serious incidents involving juvenile experimentation and simple vandalism (e.g., blowing up mailboxes). While these latter, "nuisance" incidents do have negative consequences, the committee's primary concern is those "significant" incidents that cause—or have the potential to cause—deaths, injuries, or significant property damage. Accordingly, the data in Table 1.1 were examined in order to select the actual bombings that caused at least one death, one injury, or a minimum of $1,000 in property damage. In addition, attempted bombings aimed at significant[29] targets were included.[30]

These significant actual and attempted bombing incidents involving black and smokeless powders are presented in Table 1.2. For comparison, significant actual and attempted bombing incidents involving pyrotechnics during the period 1992-1994 are shown in Table 1.3. The filtering process eliminated 59 percent of the bombings in which black powder, smokeless powder, or black powder substitutes were used, and 67 percent of the bombings in which pyrotechnics or fireworks were used.

To make an effective bomb, black powder, smokeless powder, and pyrotechnic powders must be enclosed in a container. Tables 1.2 and 1.3 also provide a breakdown of the containers used in the significant incidents involving these fillers. The type of container used in these bombs bears importantly on the ease with which these devices can be detected by various detection technologies. The data indicate that significant black and smokeless powder bombs most commonly use metal pipes, and significant pyrotechnics bombs most commonly use cardboard containers.

---

[27]Approximately 6 out of the 10 deaths and 24 out of the 100 injuries for each of the 5 years were suffered by those believed to be involved in constructing or delivering the explosive device.

[28]Committee analysis of data received from the ATF.

[29]In this context, significant targets included all targets listed in Table 1.4 except open areas and mailboxes, which were judged to have a low potential for death, injury, or significant property damage.

[30]The data made available to the committee made it possible to do this analysis only for the years 1992-1994.

TABLE 1.2   Significant Actual and Attempted Bombings Involving
Devices Using Smokeless Powder, Black Powder, or Black Powder
Substitutes

	Number of Incidents			Deaths	Injuries
	1992	1993	1994	1992-1994	1992-1994
Total incidents:	260	258	294	27	199
Actual	166	160	122	27	199
Attempted	94	98	172	—	—
Container:					
Pipe/metal	158	169	158	19	122
Pipe/plastic	28	34	43	0	16
Cardboard/paper	7	3	4	0	2
Other	60	42	72	8	53
Unknown	7	10	17	0	6

NOTE: Significant bombings represent actual bombings that caused at least one death, one injury, or a minimum of $1,000 in property damage, or attempted bombings aimed at specified targets.

SOURCE: Adapted from data received from the ATF.

TABLE 1.3   Significant Actual and Attempted Bombings Involving
Devices Using Pyrotechnics or Fireworks

	Number of Incidents			Deaths	Injuries
	1992	1993	1994	1992-1994	1992-1994
Total incidents:	130	100	142	11	267
Actual	88	72	103	11	267
Attempted	42	28	39	—	—
Container:					
Pipe/metal	17	6	14	2	13
Pipe/plastic	5	7	2	0	2
Cardboard/paper	28	35	26	3	88
Other	12	10	14	1	11
Unknown	68	42	86	5	153

NOTE: Significant bombings represent actual bombings that caused at least one death, one injury, or a minimum of $1,000 in property damage, or attempted bombings aimed at specified targets.

SOURCE: Adapted from data received from the ATF.

TABLE 1.4   Sites of Casualties Caused by Bombs Using
Propellants and Pyrotechnics Between 1992-1994

Type of Facility[a]	Deaths	Injuries
Detector installation likely		
Utilities	0	0
Government (federal)	1	2
Government (local/state)	0	0
Military	0	1
Energy facilities	0	0
Airport/aircraft	0	0
Detector installation possible		
Commercial	0	10
Educational	0	18
Police facilities	0	1
Banks	0	0
Church/synagogue	0	0
Medical facilities	0	0
Detector installation unlikely		
Residential	16	85
Apartments	3	6
Mailboxes	0	5
Vehicles	6	24
Open area	1	45
Parks	0	0
Other	0	2

[a]Facilities listed are those that are tracked by the ATF.

SOURCE: Adapted from data received from the ATF.

Targets of Bombings

The feasibility of detecting bombs prior to their explosion depends on the targets against which the bombs are directed and the method of delivery to the target. If it is not feasible to deploy a detector system at a target for routine screening, by definition a bomb will not be detected unless a detection system is directed to the scene for a specific reason—e.g., discovery of a suspicious package or receipt of a bomb threat.

Table 1.4 shows the sites at which bombs involving black powder, smokeless powder, or pyrotechnic fillers were targeted in the years 1992-1994 and the deaths and injuries caused at those sites. The targets can be grouped into three categories, depending on the feasibility of deploying bomb detection systems for routine screening at those locations. High-profile targets such as airports, utilities, or government facilities would likely be protected by such detection equipment. In the second category are establishments, such as commercial buildings, schools, and medical clinics, in which detection systems could be deployed, but only if the systems were relatively inexpensive.[31] In the third category are apartments, vehicles, and open areas where the deployment of bomb detection systems for routine screening is unlikely.

Table 1.4 shows that for the period 1992-1994, 26 out of 27 deaths and 167 out of 199 injuries caused by bombs filled with black powder, smokeless powder, or pyrotechnic compositions occurred at locations at which the deployment of detection systems for routine screening is unlikely. Thus, if these bombing patterns continue, wider deployment of routine screening technologies is unlikely to significantly affect the number of victims of black and smokeless powder bombings. Note, however, that improving the capability of law enforcement to deploy bomb detection technologies in response to an identified threat at a given site may still help to prevent casualties to bystanders and bomb squad personnel. This point is discussed further in Chapter 2.

Another factor that affects the ability to detect explosive devices using black and smokeless powders is the method by which the bombers deliver the devices to their targets. According to ATF data, the predominant method of delivery for black and smokeless powder bombs is hand placement, which was used in at least 66 percent of the 812 significant incidents that occurred in 1992-1994 (for 22 percent of the incidents, no delivery mechanism was reported).[32] It is not clear from this classification if these devices were carried into buildings (in which case a detection system at the entrance might have detected them) or were placed on the property or against an external wall. Mailed bombs that use black and smokeless powders were quite rare; the ATF data reported 19 such incidents in 1992-1994.

When a bombing incident is an act of terrorism, more people are affected than those actually injured or killed. A terrorist bombing can be defined as a premeditated act designed to cause public fear through carefully chosen acts on random and symbolic targets, including people. It is used to influence political behavior, provoke a reaction, catalyze a more general conflict, or publicize a political or ideological cause (Cannistraro and Bresett, 1998).[33] In the early 1990s, the pattern of bombing casualties and targets shown in Table 1.4 indicates that

---

[31]Detection systems that routinely screen people and packages entering a building through a controlled portal protect the people and property in the interior of the building but do not prevent the placement of a bomb on the grounds or against an exterior wall.

[32]The possible methods of delivery listed on the ATF reporting form are "placed," "mailed," "thrown," and "launched."

[33]Alternative definitions for terrorism exist. For example, 18 USC, Sec. 2332b (g)(5), states that "the term 'federal crime of terrorism' means an offense that is calculated to influence or affect the conduct of government by intimidation or coercion, or to retaliate against government conduct . . . ." Another definition of terrorism is "the unlawful use of force or violence against persons or property to intimidate or coerce a Government, the civilian population, or any segment thereof, in furtherance of political or social objectives" (FBI, 1995).

relatively few casualties occurred at locations that might be expected to be targets of terrorist attacks, e.g., aircraft, utilities, government institutions, and the like. Instead, most of the casualties occurred in private residences, vehicles, and open areas, suggesting that personal attacks on individuals, or accidents, were responsible.[34]

FINDINGS AND RECOMMENDED ACTION

Finding: *Bombs that use black or smokeless powder cause a relatively small number of deaths and injuries, but their potential for use in terrorist activity is important.* Typically over the past 5 years, about 300 "significant" bombing incidents have involved black or smokeless powder, and these bombings caused on the order of 10 deaths, 100 injuries, and $1 million in property damage annually.[35] Although the number of incidents attributed to terrorism is currently very low—in the range of one or two incidents per year—the committee notes that when bombing incidents are acts of terrorism, the target is larger than the physical location of the explosion, since a goal is to induce panic or fear among the general population. Recent examples of terrorist acts that used black and smokeless powders include the bombings of the Unabomber and the knapsack bombing in Centennial Park, Atlanta, during the 1996 Olympics.

Finding: *The databases on bombing statistics as currently compiled by two federal agencies contain serious discrepancies and are not sufficiently comprehensive.* To reach informed, appropriate decisions about legislation involving marking or tagging of explosives, policymakers need access to accurate and detailed information about the use and effects of improvised explosive devices in the United States. Currently, data are collected about the materials used in such devices, the type of target, the delivery mechanism, the number of deaths and injuries, who was killed or hurt, and the property damage. This information is valuable, and it would be useful to have, in addition, details about the final disposition of the bombing incidents (i.e., whether a suspect was identified and convicted). The data should be filed in such a way that interpretive correlations and trends in criminal activity can be readily extracted—especially for bombings judged to be "significant" according to specified criteria.

RECOMMENDED ACTION: A single, national database on bombing statistics that is comprehensive, searchable, and up-to-date should be established.

---

[34]A review of the data given in Tables 1.2 and 1.3 showed that only one incident was officially attributed to terrorism in the 3-year period. However, information on motives was not available for all of the incidents.

[35]Approximately 6 of those killed and 24 of those injured each year are perpetrators, people who are believed to have been involved in constructing or delivering the explosive device.

Both the ATF and the FBI provided the National Research Council with their data on the use of improvised explosive devices in the United States to assist the committee in understanding the extent of the problems caused by bombs involving smokeless and black powders. While this information was helpful, there were several areas in which the committee believed that more detailed and accurate statistics should be available to policymakers to allow them to make informed decisions about legislation involving the regulation, marking, or tagging of smokeless and black powders. Although both the ATF and the FBI are currently improving their systems for handling the reporting, updating, and storage of bombing data in ways that should make the data more accessible and searchable for analysts, discrepancies are likely to continue due to the agencies' different incident-reporting mechanisms and differences in the way that data exchanged between the two agencies are handled. A single form submitted[36] to a single statistics database would reduce the delays in publishing data caused by the need for reconciling data between two agencies.[37]

Much of the information needed for this statistics database must come from state and local law enforcement agencies. Therefore, a single form by which to report incidents, and incentives designed to encourage these agencies to report bombing incidents, would be useful in establishing a more accurate and complete statistics database.[38] In addition, entries should be updated as more information about an incident becomes available (such as the source of the powder used); this follow-up is particularly important for the data on suspects' identification, motivations, and convictions. In the absence of information on the resolution of bombing cases without taggants, it is difficult to assess the incremental utility that taggants would provide to law enforcement.

---

[36]Ideally, incident reports would be filed and updated online by law enforcement officers in the field and be available for online searching by analysts nationwide. The FBI Bomb Data Center is already organizing its database along these lines. Michael Fanning, FBI, personal communication, August 10, 1998.

[37]In June 1998, the most recent published bombing statistics from both the ATF and the FBI were for 1995.

[38]In 1997, the White House Commission on Aviation Safety and Security recommended that a central clearinghouse be established to compile and distribute important information relating to previously encountered explosive devices, both foreign and domestic. However, the ATF and FBI continue to maintain separate statistics databases.

Public Law 104-208 specified in 1996 that the "Secretary (of the Treasury) is authorized to establish a national repository of information on incidents involving arson and the suspected criminal misuse of explosives. All Federal agencies having information concerning such incidents shall report the information to the Secretary pursuant to such regulations as deemed necessary to carry out the provisions of this subsection. . . ."

The Uniform Federal Crime Reporting Act of 1988 states that the "Attorney General may designate the Federal Bureau of Investigation as the lead agency" to "acquire, collect, classify, and preserve national data on Federal criminal offenses as part of the Uniform Crime Reports."

X-ray display of pipe bomb. Reprinted, with permission, from the Federal Aviation Administration (FAA). Copyright 1998 by the FAA. Photo courtesy of Security Training and Technical Resources.

2

Detection of Black and Smokeless Powder Devices

INTRODUCTION

Of all the approaches to reducing bombing incidents, detecting a bomb prior to explosion is the most attractive, since it provides an opportunity to render the bomb safe before it can cause death, injury, or property damage. Fixed, portal bomb detection systems are already used to screen bags and packages coming into some highly vulnerable locations, such as airports and federal buildings. Portable x-ray detection systems and specially trained dogs are also used in responses to reports of suspicious packages or bomb threats. As mentioned in Chapter 1, however, the majority of the bombs that cause casualties or significant property damage each year in the United States explode in locations where detectors are unlikely to be deployed.[1]

Since the 1970s, researchers have investigated the possibility that special "markers" might be added to explosive materials to facilitate the detection of bombs that use these materials. This research took on a special urgency after a small quantity of plastic explosive was used to bring down a Pan American airliner over Lockerbie, Scotland, in 1989 (NRC, 1998). Plastic and sheet explosives concealed in luggage or electronic devices are difficult to detect by x-ray systems. In addition, they typically have such a low vapor pressure that they

---

[1]According to ATF data for 1992 to 1994, a total of 26 of 27 deaths and 167 of 199 injuries from propellant and pyrotechnic bombs occurred in locations where installation of detectors was deemed unlikely (see Table 1.4).

cannot be detected in a suitcase by current vapor detector technology (NRC, 1998). As a result of the Pan American tragedy, four candidate vapor markers were developed for incorporation into plastic and sheet explosives under the auspices of the U.N. International Civil Aviation Organization (ICAO) (NRC, 1998). The ICAO Convention on the Marking of Plastic Explosives for the Purpose of Detection, which was signed in 1991, was recently ratified by more than the required 35 nations and is now in effect.[2] The convention requires that all plastic and sheet explosives manufactured in the signatory nations be marked with one of the four vapor markers. These markers make the plastic and sheet explosives approximately one million times easier to detect with vapor detectors (Elias, 1991).[3]

The Committee on Smokeless and Black Powder was asked (see Appendix B) to assess the feasibility and desirability of adding markers to black and smokeless powders to enhance the likelihood of detecting explosive devices that use these powders. To evaluate the potential value of adding markers to smokeless or black powders, however, it is first important to understand the current capabilities for detecting explosive devices that use unmarked powders. The NRC report *Containing the Threat from Illegal Bombings* (NRC, 1998) reviews the relevant technologies and their application to high explosives. Rather than repeat that discussion, this report focuses only on the general classes of detection systems and their application to smokeless and black powders.

An important characteristic of bombs that use black or smokeless powders is that these powders require containment to produce an effective explosion. As discussed in Chapter 1, the purpose of the container is to confine the gases produced during the burning of the explosive powder. The resulting pressure then explodes the container, and the fragments of the container are propelled outward at high speeds to cause deaths, injuries, and property damage. The need for containment is important in detection because the containers are more easily detectable by some technologies—such as x-ray systems—than are the powder fillers themselves.[4] Thus, there are two ways to find a black or smokeless powder device: either detection of the container or detection of the powder itself. Improvised explosive devices are usually concealed in various ways, such as within

---

[2]The convention entered into force for the 38 ratifying nations on June 21, 1998. Eleven nations are capable of producing these plastic explosives, and all or most have chosen 2,3-dimethyl-2,3-dinitrobutane (DMNB) as their marking agent. James P. Rubin, State Department, press release, June 22, 1998; personal communication with Tung-ho Chen, U.S. Army, Picatinny Arsenal, Dover, N.J.

[3]The United States has mandated the addition of DMNB to all plastic and sheet explosives following the ICAO convention of 1991. Following U.S. Senate ratification of the convention in 1993, the U.S. military added DMNB to plastic explosives in 1995.

[4]By contrast, plastic explosive devices, for instance, are much harder to detect because they can cause a devastating explosion without any container. To detect these devices, it is generally necessary to detect the plastic explosive itself.

luggage or gift boxes, so that they will not be detected before they explode. Therefore, the ability of the available detection technologies to function despite this concealment must be considered.

DETECTION SCENARIOS

Three scenarios for the detection of bombs containing black and smokeless powders are considered in this report:[5]

1. *The portal scenario* applies in locations where all people or packages entering an area must pass through a few, well-monitored checkpoints. The typical example is the security checkpoint at airports.
2. *The suspicious package scenario* involves the discovery of a suspicious package in which an explosive device may or may not be concealed. An example is a box making ticking noises placed at the door of a women's health care clinic.
3. In *the bomb threat scenario*, there is reason to believe that an explosive device is somewhere within a large expanse, but the location is uncertain. For example, a person may have phoned the police to report that a bomb has been planted in a large office building. If a suspicious box or bag is located by security personnel searching the building, then the situation becomes the package scenario. This occurred in the case of the Centennial Park bombing in Atlanta in July 1996.

Note that the detection problem is not equivalent in each of the three scenarios. The portal scenario represents the classic detection problem in which a bomb must be detected with high reliability and a low false-alarm rate in the midst of a large volume of innocent items. In the suspicious package and bomb threat scenarios, attention is already directed to a specific item or area, and the challenge is to determine if that particular item or area contains a bomb. This situation would also occur in the portal scenario if the initial screening detector indicated that a particular package might contain a bomb.

These scenarios impose different requirements on detection systems. Portal systems are stationary; thus, large system size and high capital cost may be tolerable if the system has a high throughput and a low false-alarm rate. In the suspicious package and bomb threat scenarios, system portability and low cost are more important.

In some locations, such as airports and federal buildings, detection equipment is already in place to monitor incoming packages routinely for the presence

---

[5]A truck bomb or car bomb detection scenario was considered in the recent NRC report dealing with high explosives (NRC, 1998). Such a scenario is not considered relevant to black and smokeless powder bombs because of the higher cost and the containment requirements.

of bombs and other dangerous items. The available data suggest that this screening for explosives has been an effective deterrent against bombings in those areas. The presence of such equipment also acts to improve perceived public safety in these areas. If similar monitoring could be done cost-effectively and portably at all potential bombing locations, the deterrent effect could be expanded and the likelihood of bombings could be significantly reduced. However, as discussed in Chapter 1, a large number of deaths and injuries from black and smokeless powder bombs has occurred in locations for which regular screening would be technologically or practically infeasible (see Table 1.4). While much progress has been made in improving the detection of explosive materials with new technologies, current equipment can be expensive and is not always sensitive enough or appropriately configured to detect all types of devices that use the powders that are the focus of this study.

This chapter summarizes the generic classes of detection equipment and comments on their applicability to detection of various powder devices in the three scenarios described above. Potential markers are then considered in light of how they could enhance detectability in the situations in which detection of unmarked explosive devices containing black or smokeless powder is difficult. Potential problems with the markers are also discussed. The technologies commented on in this chapter are discussed in greater detail in the recent NRC report, *Containing the Threat from Illegal Bombings* (NRC, 1998). The same terminology is used in this chapter as in that study.

DETECTING IMPROVISED EXPLOSIVE DEVICES CONTAINING UNMARKED POWDERS

Assessing the desirability of adding markers to black and smokeless powders requires an understanding of current capabilities for detecting devices that use unmarked powders. Further, since large stocks of unmarked powders are available in commerce, then even if a marking program were to be initiated, it would still be important to be able to detect devices using these powders. As discussed above, the two basic ways to find a black or smokeless powder bomb are to detect the container or other bomb hardware, or to detect the black or smokeless powder within the container. The performance of current detection technologies in the scenarios of interest is summarized in Table 2.1.

Portal Scenario

A wide variety of equipment is available to detect explosives in the portal scenario, including metal detectors, x-ray machines having various levels of sophistication, and vapor/particle detection systems (NRC, 1998). In some cases, the equipment is both costly and immobile. For example, an x-ray computed tomography detector can cost as much as $900,000 and is approximately the size

TABLE 2.1   Current Detection Techniques for Unmarked Powder Devices

Detection Scenario/ Technology	Object Detected	Comments
Portal		
X-ray	Container/device	Effective, high throughput; not usable to screen for devices carried by people
Metal detector	Container/device	Effective if device contains metal; can detect devices carried by people
Vapor/particle	Powder	New technology aimed at detecting high explosives; capabilities for detecting powders not fully determined
Package		
X-ray	Container/device	Portable, lower-cost systems available for use by bomb squads; helpful in identifying presence of bomb, rendering safe, and providing evidence afterward
Metal detector	Container/device	Effective if device contains metal
Vapor/particle	Powder	Lower-cost, portable systems under development; capabilities for detecting powders not fully determined
Dogs	Powder	Effective, though exact chemicals detected by dogs and their sensitivity to powders inside well-sealed devices are not well understood
Bomb threat		
Dogs	Powder	Uniquely effective owing to both high sensitivity and self-guided searching capability

of a minivan.[6] Such machines could be used at a few high-risk locations where the portal scenario applies, but would be difficult to use in the package scenario and impossible for the bomb threat scenario.

In the case of black and smokeless powder devices, the presence of a container simplifies the detection problem considerably. The most common containers, which may be metal, plastic, glass, or cardboard, must have sufficiently strong walls to enable the buildup of the high internal pressures necessary to yield an effective bomb.[7] Thus, container walls, which typically have a higher density than either the powder fillers or the surroundings, are likely to be visible on standard x-ray systems.

---

[6]The CTX-5000 Series computed tomography detectors are roughly 14.5 feet long, 6.7 feet high, and 6.25 feet wide, and weigh approximately 9,350 pounds. Manufacturer's product literature, 1998.

[7]Note that bombers have been known to pack nails or tacks around the container to increase the number of dangerous fragments flying around when the bomb explodes. If such additions are metal, then such a device is considered for record-keeping purposes to be in a metal container, even if the powder is actually encased in some other material.

Standard x-ray machines have a high rate of throughput that makes them practical for routine screening. In addition, the effectiveness of such machines is well known publicly. Therefore, they not only serve to detect illegal devices but also merely by their presence can be a deterrent. The drawback to the use of x-ray machines at portals is the fact that they cannot be used to inspect humans because of exposure concerns. Therefore, x-ray equipment is often used in combination with metal detectors. However, while the x-ray detectors are capable of finding all sorts of containers, whether metal, plastic, glass, or cardboard, the metal detectors are limited to detecting a metal device concealed on a person, such as a pipe, nails or tacks, or a metal initiation mechanism.

Several detection systems can detect explosive vapors emanating from a device, assuming that an air sample taken near a package containing an explosive device will contain enough vapor from the explosive material to be detectable. Equipment that uses this approach includes thermo-redox detectors[8] and electron capture detectors (NRC, 1998). The size of the equipment required for sample capture and analysis is often quite large. The resulting limited mobility of the detection equipment means that such instrumentation could be used in portal and perhaps package scenarios but not in the bomb threat scenario. Other factors that could limit the effectiveness of vapor-based detection systems for devices using black and smokeless powders are the low volatility of some powders and the enclosure of the powders within pipes or other containers. The vapor pressure of single-base smokeless powders, black powders, and black powder substitutes is much lower than that of other smokeless powders,[9] and the amount of vapor expected to escape from a typical bomb container has not been established.

Several detection systems currently available can use samples obtained from the surface of a package or the handle of a bag. Such equipment includes ion-mobility-spectrometry detectors and chemiluminescence detectors (NRC, 1998). These machines are similar to those based on vapor samples except that the reliance on significant volatility of powders is removed. When a sample from the exterior of a case is tested, the assumption is that handling an explosive material or device cleanly is difficult. Very often, bomb makers will get trace elements of the powder on their hands or on the exterior of the package containing the device. Therefore, the success of such detection methods is independent of the type of container used to make the device and of the type of powder, and these detection techniques can be expected to be effective on all types of devices in the portal and package scenarios in which physical sampling of people or items is permitted. One disadvantage is the potential for false-positive alarms attributable to small

---

[8]Manufacturer's literature for the Scintrex EVD-3000.

[9]The nitroglycerin in double- and triple-base powder can be readily detected by explosives vapor detectors.

amounts of powders present on people who have had legitimate contact with such powders through reloading or manufacturing activities.

Dogs have demonstrated their ability to detect a wide range of smokeless powders, black powders, and black powder substitutes, and currently can be trained to detect devices containing any type of powder (Krauss, 1971; U.S. Department of the Treasury, 1997).[10] However, they can quickly become tired and are not well suited to the task of routine screening of large volumes of material, such as would occur in the portal situation. One technology that may hold some promise for the future is the development of an "artificial dog's nose"—an instrument that would mimic the mechanism of canine olfaction but would not be subject to fatigue. Currently, research is under way on devices that employ the molecular matching techniques thought to be utilized by dogs. While currently still in development, there is some hope that such equipment will provide a relatively low-cost, portable alternative to actual dogs.[11]

Suspicious Package Scenario

Portable standard x-ray systems are currently used to examine suspicious packages. For example, a basic portable model that can fit in the trunk of a large car and costs on the order of $20,000 is capable of providing an image of a suspicious package in real time.[12] There are several benefits of using x-ray machines in the package scenario. First, the machine constructs an image of the contents of the suspicious package that can be recorded on film and preserved or analyzed. Such an image provides information about the type of device and the location within the package that will be useful to the people in charge of preventing an incident. In addition, the picture could be used as evidence later, even if the package is destroyed in a render-safe procedure or accidental detonation. Finally, x-ray images are constructed by analyzing variations in density; therefore, x-ray equipment would be capable of detecting *any* type of powder in *any* type of container.

Vapor or residue detectors are becoming available that might be used to examine a suspicious package, but the results are likely to be less definitive than an x-ray showing the presence of a container, initiator, timer, and so forth.

The use of dogs is another detection system known to be effective in examining suspicious packages. Dogs can be trained to detect a variety of black and

---

[10]Also based on personal communications with Lyle Malotky, Federal Aviation Administration, May 12, 1998; Ed Hawkenson, U.S. Secret Service, August 7, 1998; David Kontny, Federal Aviation Administration, July 1998; and Walt Burghardt, Lackland Air Force Base, July 1998.

[11]Personal communication from Regina Dugan, Defense Advanced Research Projects Agency, May 29, 1998.

[12]Manufacturer's literature for the SAIC RTR-3.

smokeless powders. However, black and smokeless powders emit a bouquet of odors, and it is not understood to which specific chemical compounds the dogs are actually reacting and whether, once trained to detect one kind of powder, they can learn to detect another kind with a different bouquet (Rouhi, 1997). In addition, while researchers contacted by the committee have found that the operational sensitivity of dogs to small concentrations of powder vapors is quite high, their ability to detect powders in well-sealed containers, such as pipe bombs, has not been fully explored.[13] As with the portal scenario, the development of an inexpensive, portable vapor detector that would simulate a dog's nose could provide significant benefits.

Bomb Threat Scenario

At present, the only method available for searching a large area for the presence of a bomb is canine or human examination. Dogs combine high sensitivity to powders along with independent searching capability, and thus enjoy a major advantage over other detection systems in this scenario. All other systems require close proximity to the device in order to function properly. In the event that an inexpensive electronic detector were developed that would simulate the function of a dog's nose, this might provide a viable alternative.

In light of the above discussion, it is clear that of the detection technologies currently available, the standard x-ray imaging systems are the best available method for detecting devices containing unmarked explosives in the portal and package scenarios. Beyond detection, x-ray equipment also provides useful information that can assist in render-safe procedures and evidence gathering, and this equipment, when combined with metal detectors in the portal scenario, seems to be sufficient. In the bomb threat scenario, no current technologies seem to be applicable other than a thorough search by people or dogs. It is to this scenario that markers might bring the most added value.

MARKERS FOR BLACK AND SMOKELESS POWDERS

Characteristics of an Ideal Marker

The addition of markers to smokeless or black powder is designed to enhance detection, particularly through low-cost, simple systems. In assessing the value of any particular detection marker, it is useful to consider the characteristics of an ideal marker, even though such a marker may not presently be attain-

---

[13]Many pipe bombs have holes in the pipe that allow the fusing or electrical wires to be accessible to the bomber. If the holes are not completely sealed, vapor exiting such holes may facilitate canine detection of these devices.

able in practice. These criteria are not of equal importance. If the occasion for adding markers arises, choices will have to be made about which criteria are the most significant, based on the data then available.

- *No real or perceived health or safety risks.* The ideal marker would not adversely affect safety in any way. This implies that not only would it avoid changing the performance parameters of the powders, but it would also not adversely affect the health or safety of powder workers, powder users, or the general public. The ideal detection marker system would be fully accepted by the public. In addition to having no real risks, the ideal system would also have no perceived risks. The ideal system would be unobtrusive and, when implemented, would not cause significant delays or inconvenience to the public.
- *Wide applicability and utility for law enforcement.* The ideal detection marker would be applicable to all smokeless and black powder threats. It would be versatile and could be used in a wide variety of configurations and scenarios. For example, the detection marker system could be used in airports to screen passengers, carry-on items, and checked baggage. It could be used to screen vehicles passing through checkpoints such as building entrances, parking garage entrances, stadium entrances, and through freeway exits. It could be used by the U.S. Postal Service for nonintrusive scanning of mailed packages. An ideal marker system also would allow remote interrogation of suspicious packages or vehicles.
- *Chemical and physical compatibility with black and smokeless powder.* The ideal marker would be compatible with all black and smokeless powders and have no measurable effect on powder characteristics. That is, presence of the marker would have no effect on performance, safety, sensitivity, stability, shelf life, or ballistic properties. In all respects, the powder, either with or without the ideal marker, would behave in exactly the same way. See Appendix G for a discussion on the types of tests necessary for investigating chemical and physical compatibility and for a representative listing of organizations capable of conducting such tests.
- *No adverse environmental impact or contamination.* The ideal detection marker would not adversely affect the environment in any way. It would have no negative impact on the atmosphere, the soil, the water, or the food chain. The lifetime of the ideal marker would be comparable to the shelf life of black and smokeless powders; the marker would biodegrade or spontaneously disintegrate and, consequently, would not build up in the environment.
- *Low costs to various links in the chain of commerce.* The ideal marker would be inexpensive, a small fraction of the total cost of the black or smokeless powder. This low cost would include the cost of the marker itself, as well as all manufacturing, distribution, and tracking costs associated with its addition. It would be safe and simple to incorporate the marker into production of the powder and would have minimal impact on the production process. In addition, corre-

sponding detection equipment costs would be low enough to be affordable for a variety of applications (e.g., local law enforcement, train stations, building entrances). Ideally, a single marker should be used for all smokeless and black powders. A single marker simplifies detection, lowers marker cost, and lowers detection system cost. This scheme also reduces liability risks since all manufacturers mark with the same material.

• *Unique signature impossible to mask or contaminate.* The ideal detection marker would be impossible to remove or shield and would be impervious to countermeasures. With unenhanced human senses, the marked black or smokeless powder would look and smell exactly like unmarked powder. The presence of the marker would only be discernible with state-of-the-art detection technology. The marker should not be common in nature or industrial use in order to ensure that the natural background is low or nonexistent.

• *Unique information that is easy to detect.* The ideal marker would ensure that black or smokeless powder detection is straightforward and unambiguous, requiring little or no operator training or subjective evaluation. It would have sufficient signal strength (and/or background suppression) to be rapidly detected, permitting high throughput of screened objects (people or things) passing through the detection system in any orientation. The false-alarm rate would be zero, and the probability of black and smokeless powder detection would be 100 percent. Detection equipment would be portable, compact, robust, and would require little maintenance.

• *Appropriate lifetime.* In addition, the lifetime of the ideal marker would be comparable to the shelf life of the marked material. Black and smokeless powders are designed to remain functional for several decades, and, if stored properly, will last a good deal longer.

Approaches to Marking

The two basic approaches to marking powders are active marking and passive marking. Both require adding some substance or material to the powder. An active marker continuously emits some kind of signal that announces its presence; such a signal could be a chemical vapor, light, sound, radiowaves, or radioactive emissions, such as x-rays or gamma rays. An example of an active marker is an unstable atom that spontaneously decays by emitting detectable particles and/or radiation. In contrast, a passive marker must be "probed" before its presence can be detected. An example of a passive marker is a dye particle that produces visible fluorescent light when ultraviolet light is shined on the material. There are three classes of markers discussed here: active chemical vapor markers, active radiation-emitting markers, and passive markers. None of the current marking schemes are without potential difficulties. However, the various technologies are worth discussing in the context of marking powders and of enhanced detection for building or large-area searches. A more extensive description of the various marking technologies can be found in the previous NRC report (NRC, 1998).

Vapor Markers

The most obviously useful markers in the bomb threat scenario are vapor markers. Because ICAO adopted this technique for use in plastic and sheet explosives, vapor markers are the markers about which there is the most information. Double-base propellants can be readily detected by vapor detectors owing to the presence of volatile nitro compounds, such as nitroglycerin. However, the minimum amount of black powder, single-base smokeless powder, and composite propellant detectable by various detection technologies focused on powder, rather than devices, would be much lower if the powder contained an active vapor marker than if the powder were unmarked. Unlike detectors based on interrogation of powders by nuclear or x-ray radiation, vapor marker detection is applicable to all scenarios, including detection of explosives concealed on people. The effective detection of powders through detection of vapor markers could only be prevented by complex countermeasures.

Of the four markers approved for use in plastic and sheet explosives under the ICAO convention—2,3-dimethyl-2,3-dinitrobutane (DMNB), ethylene glycol dinitrate (EGDN), ortho-mononitrotoluene (*o*-MNT), and para-mononitrotoluene (*p*-MNT)—DMNB best meets the overall criteria for a suitable detection marker for high explosives, and has been added to plastic explosives in the United States since 1995.[14] DMNB is unique and apparently has no known industrial applications. There is little likelihood that this compound will be present in the background.[15] Also, relatively low levels of DMNB are readily detectable with a commercial explosive-vapor detector that is portable and low cost, coupled with the use of a proper sampling interface (ICAO, 1991). However, in considering the incorporation of DMNB into powders, there are two areas of potential concern. The first is the lifetime of DMNB, which is relatively short in comparison to the typical shelf lives of smokeless and black powders which can easily extend past 20 years. The second is introducing a substance with the toxicity level of DMNB into a commonly used material.[16]

---

[14]James P. Rubin, State Department, press release, June 22, 1998.

[15]If DMNB were to be used to mark smokeless or black powders, this might cause an increase in false alarms at bomb detection checkpoints owing to traces of the marker adhering to the millions of people who use these powders legally.

[16]The toxicity level of DMNB was a less pressing issue when it was considered for use in high explosives, which, even unmarked, have a toxicity level comparable to that of DMNB.

Radiation-emitting Markers

Among active marking alternatives to vapor markers, radiation-emitting markers—coincident gamma-ray emitters specifically—were identified as the most promising technology for marking high explosives in the 1998 NRC report. When considering the marking of smokeless and black powders, an optimal radioactive marker would emit a readily detected characteristic signature, emit sufficiently penetrating radiation to reach the detector, be detectable at levels below the natural radioactive background, have a half-life comparable to powder shelf life (which can be greater than 20 years), and be inexpensive to implement. A gamma emitter would be necessary to ensure sufficiently penetrating radiation, and the gamma rays would need to have an energy of 0.5 MeV or greater to prevent countermeasures such as shielding.[17]

Certain radioactive isotopes decay by emitting two or more gamma rays simultaneously. These isotopes are detectable at extremely low concentrations; the detectors only count events in which two gamma rays arrive within a narrow time window. Thus, isotope concentrations can be used that are actually below the natural radioactive background.

Within this category of isotopes, the three possible candidates for use as radioactive markers are the isotopes of cobalt (^{60}Co), bismuth (^{207}Bi), and sodium (^{22}Na). The 1998 NRC report noted that, of the three, ^{60}Co has the best set of characteristics for explosives marking. The isotope is available and relatively inexpensive because hospitals use sizable quantities (kilocurie amounts) as a radiation source. Also, the isotope emits a pair of nearly isotropic gamma rays with energies of 1.2 MeV and 1.3 MeV that would simplify the technical requirements for detection equipment. An important issue for marking of powders, however, is that the half-life of this isotope is 5.3 years, distinctly shorter than the expected shelf life of smokeless and black powders.[18] The half-life of ^{207}Bi (30 years) would be more suitable for powder marking; on the other hand, this isotope emits a pair of mismatched gamma rays (0.57 MeV and 1.06 MeV) that would require a pair of energy windows for each detector. Currently, the amount of research and extent of demonstrations for the ^{207}Bi marking scheme are not nearly as extensive as the work done on the ^{60}Co scheme (JASON, 1994). Note that the half-life of the positron-gamma-emitting ^{22}Na (2.6 years) is probably too short for either explosives or powder marking.

---

[17]At these energies, the amount of metal required to shield the signal becomes prohibitively large.

[18]To some extent this problem could be countered by simply adding a higher concentration of isotope to the powders. However, higher concentrations might raise health, safety, and environmental concerns.

The radiation levels caused by marking of explosive materials with radioactive isotopes would be very low—comparable to or below background.[19] However, it is worth considering not only the actual potential health impacts but also the perceived risks. The public's negative perception about radioactivity may make it exceedingly difficult to introduce such markers into a widely available commercial product.

Other Marking Approaches

Passive markers for explosives detection have been discussed in great detail in several JASON reports, although powder detection was not specifically considered (JASON, 1986, 1987, 1988, 1994). None of the passive markers that have been proposed are currently close to meeting the characteristics of the ideal marker, and the problems inherent in the majority of concepts make implementation either impossible or totally unacceptable. When discussing the potential value and difficulties involved in adding markers to smokeless and black powders, it is important to focus on the situations in which current detection of unmarked powders is insufficient or costly. Such situations include detection in the bomb threat scenario of any powder-based device, particularly one containing black or single-base smokeless powder. In this situation, portability and ease and speed of operation are of paramount importance. Therefore, for many of the passive markers the cost and size of the detection equipment preclude their usefulness. The marking techniques with expensive and unwieldy equipment include high-Z x-ray fluorescence markers, high-Z x-ray absorption edge markers, thermal neutron absorbers, and rare element nuclear magnetic resonance markers. Other passive markers—such as dipole or diode markers—are physically incompatible with powders and easily susceptible to countermeasures (JASON, 1994). Finally, a third class of passive markers—thermal neutron or deuterium markers—are so costly to purchase or to add to the powders that their consideration at this time is not practical.[20]

DISCUSSION

The committee focused its attention primarily on the applicability of vapor markers to black and smokeless powders. This choice was owing in part to the

---

[19]It has been estimated that pound for pound, bananas have three times the radioactivity (owing to naturally occurring radioactive potassium, ^{40}K) as would bulk explosives marked with ^{60}Co (JASON, 1994).

[20]Note that more details on the difficulties in all of the passive marking techniques mentioned above are given in the report *Containing the Threat from Illegal Bombings* (NRC, 1998).

availability of ICAO markers, specifically DMNB, which is currently in use in the United States for the marking of plastic and sheet explosives. In addition, in contrast to some of the other marker technologies, the committee felt that vapor markers would be applicable to each of the detection scenarios discussed in this report (see Table 2.1). The vapor markers were viewed as a possible enhancement to the capability of current systems, such as the use of dogs, to detect the more volatile components or impurities in black and smokeless powders.

The cost of marking plastic and sheet explosives with DMNB is expected to reach $0.20 per pound of explosive for marking at the 1 percent by weight level (NRC, 1998). If this same cost were applicable to powders, it would add between 1 and 2 percent to the retail cost of the powders.

As noted in Table 2.1, current portal detection systems, especially x-ray systems, are likely to be effective in detecting the containers of black and smokeless powder devices in this scenario. Accordingly, vapor markers would likely add little to detection capabilities for these devices in the portal scenario.

In the suspicious package scenario, portable x-ray systems are considered effective in detecting the device containers, and dogs are considered effective in detecting black and smokeless powders in the devices. However, the ability of dogs to detect a wide variety of different powders and their sensitivity to powders contained in well-sealed devices is not well understood. If their detection capabilities turn out to be limited in this regard, it is possible that a vapor marker could address some of these limitations. Before a marker such as DMNB could be used, however, issues relating to its loss of effectiveness over time owing to volatility, its toxicity compared to that of the powder itself, and the sensitivity of dogs to this marker would have to be addressed. A marker would also make possible the use of a vapor detector tuned to detect that specific marker.

In the bomb threat scenario, the only detection options currently available are searches by humans or dogs. Canine searches are likely to be effective, subject to the potential limitations discussed above in the package scenario. The presence of a marker might enhance the speed with which a canine could locate a bomb, or in the future make possible the use of a vapor-sniffer device (artificial dog's nose) that could facilitate the search by following a concentration gradient of the vapor marker to the device's location.

The benefits of a marking program are limited by bombers' ability to obtain unmarked powders, either from existing stockpiles, or by manufacturing the powders themselves from precursor chemicals. Given the large volumes of commercial and military surplus powders available and their long shelf life (at least 20 years), even if a full-scale marking program were implemented today by powder manufacturers, potential bombers would have access to unmarked powders for many years to come. Clandestine manufacture of black powder from its constituent chemicals would provide another way of evading a marking program.

FINDINGS AND RECOMMENDATIONS

The detection of improvised explosive devices that contain black and smokeless powders must be considered in the context of the materials that are used to make the devices and the situations in which the devices are used.

Finding: Pipe bombs and similar explosive devices that use black and smokeless powders can be detected by exploiting both the properties of the powder itself and those of the container.

Finding: Current x-ray systems are capable of detecting explosive devices containing black and smokeless powders and are effective when placed at a portal or when used in portable equipment to examine a suspicious package. Current x-ray technologies are not suitable for quickly screening large numbers of packages or for performing large-area searches. This method of detection has the advantages that the x-ray image provides information about the construction of the device that can be useful in render-safe procedures, and the image can be preserved on film to be used as evidence in an investigation or prosecution. Thus, x-ray systems are very useful in portal scenarios, such as for examination of the packages that come into a company mailroom or that are carried onto a plane.[21] Portable x-ray machines can also be carried to the location of a suspicious package and used to determine its contents.

The limitations of x-ray equipment relate to its weight and method of analysis. Because the current portable x-ray detectors are roughly double the size of a large suitcase and must be set up around a specific package, x-ray technology is of limited use when searching large open areas or buildings in response to a bomb threat. Also, x-ray images must be examined by trained personnel or require the use of complex pattern recognition software to determine if the contents of the package resemble an explosive device. That is, this technology cannot be effective for screening large numbers of packages, as would be needed for example, to examine all baggage or mail shipped by airlines or all packages transported by a commercial delivery service.

Finding: Both black and smokeless powders contain volatile compounds that are detectable by dogs. Canine searches are the only viable means of conducting large-area searches for hidden explosive devices. Dogs are used by the U.S.

---

[21]For health reasons, x-ray equipment cannot be used to screen people entering through a portal; instead, metal detectors are used for this purpose. However, unlike x-ray systems that enable security personnel to view an image of the interior of a package and therefore detect a wide array of devices, metal detectors can only indicate metal objects concealed on a person and therefore are only able to detect devices that utilize metal containers or include other metallic components. Thus, metal detectors are more easily circumvented than x-ray systems.

Secret Service, the Bureau of Alcohol, Tobacco, and Firearms, and the Federal Aviation Administration to detect explosive materials. They are also used by bomb-scene technicians to help investigators locate powder evidence that may not be visible to humans. The experience of the agencies that train such dogs and study their abilities has demonstrated that the dogs are capable of recognizing the presence of black and smokeless powders. However, there is not complete understanding of the biochemical mechanism of canine olfaction, the circumstances that can interfere with canine detection of powders, or the exact chemicals and concentration of chemicals that dogs are able to detect.

RECOMMENDED ACTION: Further research should be conducted on canine detection of bombs made with black and smokeless powders enclosed in various containers. Research should also be conducted on the development of inexpensive and portable instrumental sensors that mimic canine detection.

Better knowledge of how dogs detect devices containing black and smokeless powders would enable more efficient and appropriate use of dogs in examining large areas and buildings and would assist in the development of instruments capable of mimicking the methods by which dogs detect powders. Depending on their size, cost, and speed, such instruments could be used for large-area searches and for high-throughput, routine screening of packages.

Finding: *Detection markers added to black and smokeless powders could assist in the detection of explosive devices in several situations: large-area searches, examination of suspicious packages, rapid and routine screening of large numbers of packages, and enhancement of canine ability to detect black and smokeless powder bombs.* A detection marker's value to law enforcement for detecting explosive devices containing black and smokeless powder would depend on the properties of the added marker, such as its degree of detectability through a sealed pipe or layers of wrapping, and on the portability and cost of the associated detection equipment, as well as its range and sensitivity.

Finding: *No current marking system has been demonstrated to be technically feasible for use in black and smokeless powders.* While vapor markers have been successfully introduced into plastic and sheet explosives, there has not been a definitive study of how such markers might work in black and smokeless powders. Some issues of concern include the high volatility and the toxicity of vapor markers such as DMNB. In marking techniques that use radiation-emitting isotopes such as cobalt-60, the concentration of isotope required to produce the desired detection sensitivity has not been established. A potential limitation of such a marking system is the public's negative view of radiation, even at low levels, as well as the technique's suitability for use only in the portal scenario, owing to the costly and nonportable nature of the associated detection equipment.

RECOMMENDATION: Detection markers in black and smokeless powder should not be implemented at the present time.

X-ray systems and dogs currently provide a strong capability for detecting bomb containers and unmarked black and smokeless powders in the scenarios considered by the committee, and most powder bombings currently take place at locations in which deployment of bomb detection systems is not practicable (see Table 1.4). Therefore, the committee believes that the effectiveness of a marking program would be limited at the present time. Institution of a marking program would incur significant costs. At the current level of fewer than 10 deaths and 100 injuries per year and very few terrorist incidents, the committee believes that the benefits are not sufficient to justify such a marking program. If the threat were to increase substantially in the future, and test data were available, benefits might exceed costs, and a marking program might be warranted. A marking program for black and smokeless powders would be justified only if three criteria were met: the frequency and severity of black and smokeless powder bombs were found to be high enough to justify marking; the markers first were thoroughly tested and found to be safe and effective under conditions likely to be encountered in the legal and illegal uses of the powders; and the social benefits of markers were found to outweigh the costs of their use.

RECOMMENDED ACTION: Research should be conducted to develop and test markers that would be technically suitable for inclusion in black and smokeless powders. The marking schemes studied should be those that would assist in large-area searches or rapid screening of a large number of packages.

More information and work are needed on marking technologies. Should it become necessary for policymakers to mandate the implementation of more intensive control procedures, the agencies concerned would then have the data necessary to make informed decisions about markers.

Reconstruction of exploded pipe bomb. Reprinted, by permission, from the U.S. Postal Inspection Service. Copyright 1998 by the U.S. Postal Inspection Service.

3

Identification

INTRODUCTION

After a bombing takes place, much information about the improvised explosive device can be obtained through careful processing of the bomb scene. In bombing incidents in which black or smokeless powder is used, bomb components recovered may include unreacted or partially burned powder, chemical products of the reaction, and parts of the device, such as the container used to contain the powder, the container used to transport the device, triggering or delay mechanisms, and adhesive tape. Identifying and tracing the origin of these components, including the brand and product line of the smokeless or black powder used in a bombing, may aid in identifying and eventually convicting the bomber. The Committee on Smokeless and Black Powder was specifically charged with determining whether taggants, added to black or smokeless powder, would substantially assist law enforcement personnel in identifying, apprehending, and convicting bomb makers.[1]

Identification taggants are coded materials that can be added to a product by the manufacturer to provide information that can be "read" by investigators at some later stage in the use of the product. Taggants are currently added by manufacturers to a variety of products, such as gasoline, construction materials, and perfume, to enable detection of product tampering or counterfeiting.[2] These

---

[1] See Appendix B for the statement of task.

[2] Some commercial applications of taggants for prevention of counterfeiting and for product identification are given by Schlesinger (1998).

commercial examples may provide useful guidance regarding addition of taggants to smokeless or black powder, although their information content is limited (they need only be identifiable) and they are not designed to withstand explosions.

As a first step in assessing the value of adding taggants to black or smokeless powder, current investigatory methods used by law enforcement personnel are summarized, especially the role of physical evidence in bombing cases. Methods for identifying the powder used in a bomb, such as the use of powder databases, as well as the ability to trace black or smokeless powder from manufacturer to last legal purchaser, have implications that will affect the decision to add taggants. If taggants are to be effective, they must substantially enhance the steps in an investigation and lead to faster apprehension and more certain conviction of the perpetrators.

An additional factor is the nature of the taggant itself. The committee found it helpful to list criteria for an ideal taggant, not only to assess the state of current technology but also to provide guidance for design of new taggant technologies.

Currently, Switzerland is the only country where taggants are added to explosives. This program includes the tagging of black powder, but only that used for blasting purposes. Neither smokeless nor black powder for shooting purposes is tagged. The relevance of the Swiss experience has been carefully assessed in considering the addition of taggants to smokeless and black powder in the United States.

METHODS AND APPROACHES

The Role of Physical Evidence in Bombing Cases

The utility of adding taggants to propellant powders rests on the incremental benefits they may offer to law enforcement in the context of all the physical and chemical evidence available in a given case. A primary focus of forensic laboratory examination of postblast evidence is to analyze chemical residues in order to identify the explosive and provide investigators with as much information as possible about its probable origin. Identifying the explosive, however, is but one part of a comprehensive examination process; to better understand the scope of such an investigation, it is instructive to examine typical components of an improvised explosive device and the nature of evidence left after an explosion.

A smokeless or black powder improvised device consists of a number of components, including some or all of the following: powder, a container to confine the powder, delivery and concealment means (bag, parcel, and the like), an ignition mechanism, and a timing or victim-initiated mechanism (see Figure 3.1).

Other sources of physical evidence can include material designed to injure or kill (e.g., nuts and bolts, screws, nails, and metal staples) and packaging material (e.g., wood or cardboard boxes). Such components can result in potentially valuable physical evidence being recovered at the crime scene; examples include

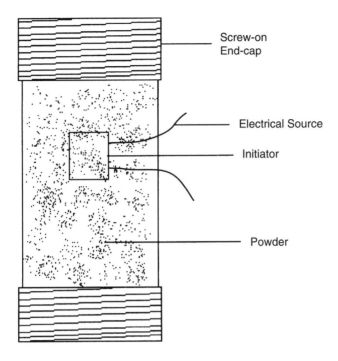

Screw-on
End-cap

Electrical Source

Initiator

Powder

FIGURE 3.1   Pipe bomb.   SOURCE: Adapted from Scott (1994).

fragments of the container, unburned powder, pieces of the packaging, lengths of safety fuse, wires, springs, initiators, fragments of batteries, fragments of clocks, and the like. Any of the components of an improvised explosive device potentially may be used to associate the device with its builder. One example is the specialty nails recovered at the scene of the Centennial Park bombing. Approximately 6 pounds of 8d nails, called "concrete" or "masonry" nails, were used in the bomb. Both the type of nail and the amount purchased were unusual. As a result, the Federal Bureau of Investigation (FBI) requested that individuals with knowledge of such a purchase contact the FBI.[3]

Propellant powders are normally designed to function by very rapid burning rather than by detonation. Frequently, unreacted smokeless powder granules are thrown out of an exploding device and can be recovered at the bomb scene. Less often, unreacted black powder can be located similarly, but characteristic residue is nearly always present after black powder bombings (in the absence of water). Information about the powder used in a bomb supplements the data about the

---

[3]FBI press statement, November 18, 1997.

many other kinds of physical evidence typically present at a bomb scene to assist investigators in identifying a suspect and linking the individual to the crime.

Black Powder

Unreacted black powder consists of irregularly shaped granules coated with graphite, giving the granules a distinctive black and glossy appearance when observed through a microscope. As discussed in Chapter 1, the typical composition contains charcoal, sulfur, and potassium nitrate (or occasionally sodium nitrate). Black powder is not a very efficient explosive in that a large percentage of its products are condensed solids rather than gases (AB Bofors Nobelkrut, 1960). This does, however, give forensic scientists an advantage in that black powder, even if entirely consumed, yields significant quantities of characteristic residue (Mohanty, 1998; Bender, 1998). The primary intrinsic characteristics of black powder are its morphology, composition, and the large quantity of residue produced by burning or explosion.

Smokeless Powder

Only single- and double-base smokeless powders (see Chapter 1) are normally encountered in explosive devices.[4] As noted previously, smokeless powders contain small amounts of chemical additives, such as stabilizers or flash suppressants; these substances may be identified during the postblast chemical analyses of powders or residues.

Smokeless powders generally have a graphite surface coating and are produced in more regular shapes than black powder. Common shapes include flattened balls, tubes, and disks. An important part of the forensic examination of smokeless powders involves the careful measurement of the granule dimensions (Figure 3.2) either with a microscope equipped with a calibrated micrometer eyepiece or an image profiler. Recently, the National Laboratory Center of the Bureau of Alcohol, Tobacco, and Firearms (ATF) has begun to explore the use of digital image capture and digital image analysis to replace these labor-intensive ways of measuring granule dimensions (Bender, 1998).

---

[4]Only single- and double-base powders are available commercially; triple-base powders and composite propellants are manufactured for special applications, such as large-caliber military weapons or air bag inflators.

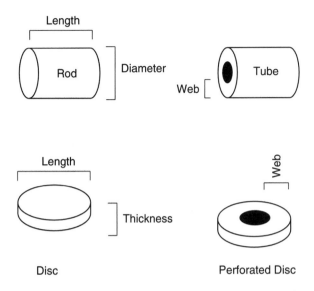

FIGURE 3.2   Physical characteristics of various types of smokeless powder. SOURCE:
Adapted from Bender (1998).

Use of Black and Smokeless Powder Databases

The FBI Chemistry Unit Laboratory and the National Laboratory Center of
the ATF have each devoted considerable effort to accumulating data on the
physical dimensions and chemical composition of different types of smokeless
powders (see Appendix F) for use in forensic investigations to identify smokeless
powder. The creation and maintenance of these two powder databases require the
commitment of laboratory resources to accomplish a variety of tasks: liaising
with powder manufacturers and distributors to obtain samples of new products,
accumulating samples of different lots of powder, analyzing physical dimensions
and morphologies of the smokeless powder granules, analyzing the chemical
composition of representative samples of the smokeless powders, and entering
these data into a computerized powder database (Wallace and Midkiff, 1993;
Bender, 1998). Because of the pressure of casework and the limited human and
financial resources available for this activity, the powder databases maintained
by the FBI and ATF are incomplete.[5]

---

[5]Personal communication, Cynthia Wallace, ATF, March 19, 1998, and Ron Kelley, FBI, March
19, 1998.

Although both the FBI Chemistry Unit Laboratory and the National Laboratory Center of the ATF are able to identify the type of smokeless powder used in a bombing or in an unexploded device in the majority of cases, both laboratories nevertheless do encounter smokeless powder samples that are not in their powder databases. In such cases, valuable time may be lost at the beginning of an investigation because of the need to visit powder manufacturers to solicit their technical staffs' assistance in identifying the powder. In some cases, the origin of the smokeless powder used in a bombing or attempted bombing may remain undetermined. Analysts at both the FBI Chemistry Unit Laboratory and the National Laboratory Center of the ATF expressed the belief that the addition of taggants could aid them by providing the ability to identify the manufacturer and product line of a smokeless powder, especially in those instances in which conventional analytical methods now fail.[6]

In forensic investigations of black powder, the granule size is the main characteristic examined.[7] The FBI and ATF keep samples and/or information about the physical dimensions of various commercially available black powders. These samples and data are available for use in comparisons with evidence from bomb scenes. Both agencies agreed that information about the chemical composition of the different black powders has little evidentiary value.

Tracing the Product Through the Distribution Chain

Taggants may be used to identify the manufacturer and product line of smokeless or black powder used in a bomb without additional record keeping on the part of the manufacturer or retailer. For example, the dyed powder granule that Alliant Techsystems adds to some of its smokeless powder allows the user to identify immediately the specific product line (Red Dot, Blue Dot, Green Dot). However, establishing an additional audit trail would be necessary to enable law enforcement personnel to trace a particular powder used in a bomb from the manufacturer to the last legal purchaser. At each stage in the distribution system, sellers would have to record which tagged powders were sent to which customers, and retail outlets would have to keep their sales records in a form that could be readily accessed by investigators. To examine the issues raised by such a record-keeping system, the committee reviewed the existing system of normal business records kept in the manufacture, distribution, and retail selling of powders.[8] Three types of records could be kept in the current system: records within

---

[6]Site visits to the ATF and the FBI (see Appendix F) and subsequent discussions with laboratory personnel, August 19, 1998.

[7]Personal communication, Cynthia Wallace, ATF, June 24, 1998.

[8]For the purposes of this study, analysis of record keeping was limited to black and smokeless powder sold commercially for reloading purposes. Other applications of black and smokeless powders include use in commercial ammunition and specialized military devices, among others. However, the volume of production for commercial ammunition is tremendous, and the array of military

a manufacturing or distribution facility, records tracking the movement of powder between such facilities, and records at the retail level that identify the purchaser.

Current Record Keeping in the Powder Distribution System

Details of the record-keeping process were provided by a company that both packages its own powder and repackages powders made by other companies;[9] the record-keeping procedures were not expected to vary widely throughout the powder industry. In repackaging powders, each 1-pound (or larger) canister of powder is stamped with a date of packing and a lot number. This stamp also goes on the packing boxes that hold the powder containers. Records of the amount packaged, date, and lot number are maintained indefinitely. However, once the powder is shipped from the repackaging facility to either master distributors or retailers, the chain of record keeping ends, and a record of the final destination of the canisters packaged on a given day from a specific lot does not exist.

At the next level of the distribution system, master distributors receive powder from the original manufacturers or repackagers and supply it to smaller distributors and retail outlets (see Figure 1.1 in Chapter 1). Again, records are maintained by the master distributors about the type and quantity of powder on their property, but distribution beyond their facility is not tracked.[10]

For comparison, the system for tracking high explosives in the United States is more rigorous. In the United States, packaged commercial high explosives are required to be marked with a bar code that indicates the manufacturer and the date and shift on which the explosive was manufactured. These date and shift codes have proven to be useful both in tracing the disposition of purchased explosives and in investigating attempted bombings involving these packaged explosives. Sometimes these packaging markings survive a bomb blast.

---

applications for black and smokeless powders is immense. As a result, tracking the disposition of a specific lot of powder through the distribution system to the final use of the ammunition or military device would be very difficult. In addition, the relatively high cost and difficulties involved in obtaining quantities of black or smokeless powder sufficient for use in an improvised explosive device from military devices or ammunition also remove these sources from the main focus of this study.

[9]Information supplied to the subcommittee during its visit to Hodgdon Powder Company; see Appendix F.

[10]When large quantities of black or smokeless powder (over 100 pounds) are transported, the powder is shipped as an explosive, and Department of Transportation regulations require more detailed documentation about the shipment. These records might be helpful in tracking the location of black powder, but they are not currently coupled with the record-keeping procedures within individual manufacturing, packaging, or distribution facilities. Smaller quantities of black powder and most smokeless powder are shipped as flammable solids and are subject to less strict federal regulations.

Current Record Keeping at the Retail Level

One potential advantage of a tagging program would be to enable investigators to obtain information leading to the last legal purchaser of the tagged powder used in a bombing. This would require that retail outlets maintain records of which customers purchased which tagged powders. Even in the absence of a tagging program, however, several forensic investigators contacted by the committee indicated that it would be useful in bombing investigations to be able to obtain from local retailers a list of individuals who had recently bought the same type of powder used in the bombing.[11] The committee therefore attempted to characterize the current state of record keeping for the retail sale of powders.

Federal Requirements

Retail purchases of black powder are not regulated for quantities below 50 pounds (Code of Federal Regulations, 1981). Purchases of black powder above 50 pounds are regulated by the ATF in the same way as high explosives: for intrastate or contiguous state use, the purchaser must fill out a form, which is retained by the seller. For interstate transport and use, the purchaser must have a federal license or permit. There are no federal regulations concerning the retail sale of smokeless powders.

State and Local Requirements

Many states have legislation that regulates the purchase or possession of explosive materials, but the great majority have exempted from licensing requirements small amounts of black or smokeless powder, or all black and smokeless powder that is acquired for personal or recreational use (see Appendix H on state laws). Five states have regulatory legislation that places some restrictions on the purchase of small quantities of black or smokeless powders. California has by far the most detailed scheme.[12] Three other states, Illinois, Massachusetts, and Michigan, and the District of Columbia require some form of license in order to purchase, possess, or reload powder.[13] Mississippi and Virginia require some record keeping on the part of the sellers.[14] Although there is no way of knowing the impact of such controls on potential bombers, the committee is aware of anec-

---

[11]Personal communication from Richard Strobel and Cynthia Wallace, ATF, during a site visit to the ATF National Laboratory Center, March 19, 1998. See Appendix F for more information.

[11]See Cal. Health & Safety Code § 12102.1

[13]See D.C. Code Ann. § 6-2341(a); Ill. Ann. Stat. Ch. 225, § 210/1004; Mass. Gen. L. ch. 140, § 131(E); and Mich. Comp. Laws, ch. 140, § 129(C).

[14]See Miss. Code Ann. § 45-13-101; Va. Code Ann. § 59.1-138.

dotal evidence that law enforcement investigators visit retail establishments to determine whether there is any record keeping that might provide leads to bombing suspects.[15] Implementation of a uniform record-keeping requirement for all states would require action by Congress.

TAGGANTS FOR BLACK AND SMOKELESS POWDERS

While an initial examination of the current state of the art of forensic investigations of bombings indicates that taggants would assist in such investigations, the effects of adding taggants to black and smokeless powders must be carefully examined. Consideration of the characteristics of an ideal taggant helps to clarify the issues involved.

Characteristics of an Ideal Taggant

Ideal characteristics are by their nature unattainable, but, by establishing these criteria, proposed taggant concepts may be judged against agreed-upon characteristics. If a significant increase in threat from the illegal use of black and smokeless powder demands quick implementation of a taggant system, reasonable concession may have to be made in the selection of a taggant in order to increase overall public safety. The ideal taggant would have the following characteristics, which are not necessarily of equal importance:

• *No real or perceived health or safety risks.* The ideal taggant poses no safety risk. It is inert. It does not in any way affect the normal properties of the energetic material in which it is admixed nor does it adversely affect the health or safety of powder workers, powder users, or the general public. The ideal taggant is fully accepted by the public. In addition to posing no real risks, the ideal taggant has no perceived risks. It is unobtrusive and manifests no inconvenience to the end users of the black and smokeless powders nor to the general public.

• *Wide forensic applicability and utility for law enforcement.* The ideal taggant is applicable to all black and smokeless powder threats. It can provide unambiguous, detailed information to law enforcement agents concerning the manufacture and distribution of powders used in a crime. Law enforcement agents with only modest training and relatively unsophisticated equipment can obtain this information. The ideal taggant is not a source of cross-contamination, and its intrinsic value is not adversely affected by other sources of contamination. The ideal taggant would not only be recoverable from unburned powder, but would also survive a blast in which all the powder had been consumed.

---

[15]Personal communication to subcommittee during its site visit to the ATF, March 19, 1998, and to the FBI, March 19, 1998; see Appendix F.

• *Chemical and physical compatibility with black and smokeless powders.* The ideal taggant is compatible with all black and smokeless powders and has no measurable effect on the powder's material properties nor its performance characteristics. For example, the presence of the taggant has no effect on performance, safety, sensitivity, stability, shelf life, or ballistic properties. In all respects, the behavior of a black or smokeless powder with or without the ideal taggant is indistinguishable.

• *No adverse environmental impact or contamination.* The ideal taggant does not affect the environment in any way. It has no negative impact on the atmosphere, the soil, the water, or the food chain. The lifetime of the ideal taggant is comparable to the shelf life of the properly stored black or smokeless powder in which it is incorporated. Upon exposure to the elements, the taggant will naturally biodegrade or spontaneously decompose so that there is no environmental accumulation.

• *Low cost to various links in the chain of commerce.* The ideal taggant is comparatively inexpensive, representing a small fraction of the total cost of the smokeless or black powder in which it is used. This low cost includes the cost of the taggant itself, as well as all manufacturing, distribution, and tracking costs associated with the addition of the taggant. It is safe and simple to incorporate into production of the powders and has minimal, if any, impact on the production process. In addition, the attendant decoding equipment costs are low enough to be affordable to all law enforcement agencies.

• *No viable countermeasures.* The ideal taggant is exceedingly difficult to remove from the powder in which it is incorporated. The tagged smokeless or black powder looks, smells, feels, and behaves materially exactly like the untagged powder. The presence of the ideal taggant can be discerned only with appropriate equipment, but detection does not facilitate its removal from the powder. The information encoded in the taggant cannot be compromised or destroyed. The ideal taggant is not found in nature nor in common usage in industry. The presence of the ideal taggant at a crime scene is unequivocally indicative of the involvement of black or smokeless powders.

• *Unique information that is easy to read.* An ideal taggant provides unique information on the manufacturer and chain of custody of each black and smokeless powder in which it is incorporated. Gleaning this information is dependent upon the availability of reading and decoding equipment and applicable powder databases. The ideal taggant can provide useful information to each level (field to laboratory) involved in a forensic investigation.

Taggant Technologies

A large number of companies and other organizations proposed taggant concepts that were considered by this committee (see Appendix D). One of these taggant technologies (the 3M-type taggant) has been used since 1981 in explosives in Switzerland.[16] Some of the existing taggant technologies have been used in applications not related to explosives, such as animal feeds, perfume, personal hygiene products, and gasoline. Because many of these industries use taggants as a means to combat counterfeiting, the need to change the taggant code periodically is not as crucial as it would be in the smokeless and black powder industry.

Many of the taggant technologies presented to the committee remain in the conceptual stage, and extensive research, development, and testing would be required before the taggant would be a viable commercial product. If one of these underdeveloped technologies were chosen for use in tagging black and smokeless powder, immediate implementation would not be possible since extensive testing would need to be performed.

Taggant Classification

To understand better the potential features and limitations of proposed taggants, the committee developed a classification scheme for taggant technologies. The two general types of taggants, referred to as Class I and Class II, are discussed below, along with the criteria for ideal taggants identified above, in terms of their application to black powder and smokeless powder. The results are summarized in Table 3.1.

• *Class I. Single entity.* All coded information is contained within a single structural entity (this could be a macroscopic particle, a microscopic particle, or an individual molecule). The taggant cannot be subdivided, and the information content can be compromised only by destruction of the structural entity (i.e., the particle or molecule). This structural entity could be a particle of the material that is being tagged, or it could be a foreign particle that is mixed with the powder.
• *Class II. Multicomponent.* The coded information is provided by the presence or absence (and perhaps also by relative amounts or ratios) of several species that can be added individually to the material to be tagged. The information content can be compromised by selective removal or destruction of one or more components—or by adding any of these components (for example, by mixing with material that is tagged with a different coding ratio). Because the information content depends on relative quantities (or the presence or absence) of several components, it is essential to obtain a statistically valid sample at the crime scene.

Any taggant concept can be designed as either Class I or Class II, and methods of analysis would be similar. Class II taggants are more vulnerable to countermeasures. If identification occurs by determining the ratio of the compo-

---

[16]The taggants currently used in Switzerland are manufactured by Microtrace and sold to 3M, which sells them to manufacturers in Switzerland.

TABLE 3.1   Classification and Summary of Proposed Taggant Concepts

Taggant Type	Examples	Comments
Class I—Resistant to countermeasures: mixing could enhance information content rather than destroy taggant code		
1. Physical	3M, Microtrace	Used in Switzerland for explosives, including black powder for blasting
	Explotracer, HF6	Used in Switzerland for high explosives only
	Microdot	No data available
2. Spectroscopic	Organic dyes (e.g., Alliant Red Dot)	Currently used in smokeless powder
	Lanthanide (encapsulated)	Original Westinghouse taggant
3. Chemical	Biomolecules (proteins, DNA)	Used in inks, pharmaceuticals
4. Isotopic	Taggant added in which each "particle" has identical isotopic substitution	No proposed use
Class II—May be susceptible to countermeasures: mixing products could destroy code		
1. Physical	Microbeads	Used in animal feeds
2. Spectroscopic	Lanthanides	
3. Chemical	Mixture of molecules added	
4. Isotopic	Isotag LLC method using known, random ratios of deuterated compounds	Inexpensive, isotopic mixtures
	Specific labeling	Used in biochemical trace analysis; expensive

nents in the taggant, mixing two powder canisters containing a Class II taggant that has two different codes presumably would destroy the taggant information. However, with some of the smaller taggant particle sizes, many taggant particles might adhere to the surface of the larger powder granules, effectively behaving like a Class I taggant. Another consideration is the loss in information that may occur when a Class II taggant is part of an explosive mixture. In an explosion, different components burn at different rates. Loss of information will occur if the different components of the Class II taggant degrade at different rates. Aside from these concerns about countermeasures and information loss, the advantages and disadvantages for Class I and Class II taggants would be similar. (Note that practically any Class II taggant could be converted to Class I by encapsulation.)

Taggants (Class I and II) can be subdivided into four categories, according to the way that the taggant information is encoded.

1. *Physical.* The coding results from physically (or optically) observable properties of the taggant. Class I examples would include Microtrace taggants and miniature "bar code" particles (or some other type of particle with miniaturized "writing"). An example of Class II would be a mixture of different sizes (and/or colors) of glass microspheres.

2. *Spectroscopic.* The coding results from the absorption or emission characteristics of the taggant. Class I examples include particles containing some combination of dyes or lanthanides, including dyes applied directly to individual granules of the powder. Class II examples include addition of a mixture (not encapsulated) of the same dyes or lanthanides to the powder.

3. *Chemical.* The coding corresponds to the chemical structures of the individual taggant molecules, and the code is read by determining the molecular structure. Class I examples include biomolecules such as DNA or proteins, where each molecule contains the full code (which is read by some combination of biological and instrumental techniques). Class II examples include mixtures of compounds in which the code could be read by instrumental analysis.

4. *Isotopic.* This type of coding results from isotopic labeling of one of the components of the powder (usually analyzed by mass spectroscopic techniques). Class I examples would use site-specific isotopic labeling of components of the powder. Class II examples include the Isotag LLC approach of adding a randomly generated (but unique) mixture of deuterium-labeled compound that has a characteristic fingerprint when analyzed by gas chromatography/mass spectrometry.

Evaluation of Taggant Concepts Against Ideal Characteristics

Using all available data, the committee grouped and evaluated proposed taggant concepts according to the stated ideal technical characteristics. As stated above, no taggant technology could be developed that fully meets each of these ideal criteria. But if these criteria were considered as a continuum, then it would be possible to implement a taggant that meets at least some minimum qualification for each of these categories.

The following section describes the issues that arise when considering taggant concepts against each of the ideal characteristics listed above in this chapter. The discussion is not specific to any particular taggant concept, and therefore broad general questions are raised, not all of which would be applicable to all taggant concepts. To illustrate the application of the ideal taggant criteria in a specific scenario, an example of a particular taggant concept and some of the associated research questions are presented in Box 3.1.

**BOX 3.1 An Example of a Tagging Scenario and Related
Research Questions**

Research on taggants represents the study of a complex system into which
some unique material is introduced (the taggant). This material has only one function—to retain information that can survive a bomb blast, typically by being thrown
out of the immediate zone of the explosion (along with unconsumed powder) in the
course of the release of pressure during bomb-container rupture. The taggant in
such a system might carry a variety of information that would allow law enforcement personnel to trace the bomb back to the perpetrator and support the prosecution of the bomber.

The following example illustrates some of the research, technological, and forensic questions that need to be addressed to provide sufficient understanding of
the use of taggants in black and smokeless powders before a tagging program
could be instituted. Taggants could consist of a selected, large number of unique
entities that might provide such information as manufacturer, product type, and lot
number. These entities could use the following types of labels: various gene se-
quences; different isotopic ratios of the major powder constituents; or small mi-
cron-sized particles of different sizes, composition, and color. Using combinations
of these entities, every can of smokeless and black powder potentially could have
a unique combination. An appropriate record-keeping system would have to be in
place to track the combinations of taggants in each container of the powder.

Sample Scenario

In one possible scenario, taggants on the order of 5 microns in size could be
added to powder consisting of propellant granules roughly 500 microns in diameter
at 0.02 percent by mass (assuming equal densities for taggants and the powder
granules). The taggants could be added to the canister either concurrently during
filling with powder or after filling with powder. In this situation, an individual powder

---

No Real or Perceived Health or Safety Risks

The potential for health and safety risks can be considered for two different
groups that might be affected: industry workers and end users. In both cases, any
potential toxicity or health effects caused by the taggant material must be considered, and, for industry workers, any potential increase in the hazards of the manufacturing process caused by the inclusion of taggants must also be examined.

Biological or chemical materials would be used as taggants only if they do
not produce adverse health effects. The "biological" materials that have been
suggested for use as taggants could be synthetic materials rather than materials
found in nature. Consequently, they would be designed in such a way that no
adverse human health effects would be expected. In the case of chemical agents,
it would be necessary to establish that any possible toxicity of an added taggant,

granule could have between 100 and 1,000 taggants adhered to its surface. The technical questions listed below could be raised about such a system.

Statistical Uniformity of the Taggant Information Throughout the Powder Sample

- After thorough mixing, what is the distribution of taggants within the container?
- Does each propellant particle contain a statistically representative ratio of the individual taggants?
- What is the distribution of taggants on a propellant particle for the case where two or more cans of propellants are mixed?

Effect on Legitimate Use of Black and Smokeless Powders

- Do the taggants affect the velocity and pressure developed in the gun?
- What is the level at which there is no measurable effect on such parameters?
- At the no-effect level, is there sufficient taggant on the particle such that a taggant system is still effective?
- What is the lifetime of the various tagging systems? Would the relevant taggant properties persist over the course of 10, 20, or 50 years?
- Do the taggants affect the function of guns or their lifetime?

Usefulness in Forensic Investigation After the Bomb Blast

- What is the survivability of the taggants?
- If different types of taggants (i.e., various colors of particles) are adhering to the particles, is the ratio of types on a recovered powder granule the same as the original ratio at which the taggant was added?
- How would the analysis of the evidential powders from a bomb site be performed to provide unequivocal identity of the powder?

or its associated combustion products, would not increase the health risks above any inherent risks posed by the powder itself.

Potential methods of exposure for users include the handling of tagged powders as well as breathing any fumes from the powder or reaction products that are produced in use, such as during the firing of a gun. Thus, the safety of any additives to such powders must be looked at from this perspective. This is not the case with taggants in high explosives where the use of such materials is remote from any operating personnel. Another potential area of concern would be whether the taggants affected the stability of powder in storage. It is possible that any new taggant used with black or smokeless powder could be shown to pose health or safety risks at very high concentrations of the taggants within the powder. However, when assessing the risks that the taggant may add to the use or manufacture of black or smokeless powder, the actual concentrations at which the taggant would be added must be a consideration.

The greatest safety risk during manufacture has been suggested to be the potential for explosion caused by friction associated with a particulate material that might be used as a taggant. The relative hardness and abrasive qualities of a multilayer acrylic particle (a Microtrace-type taggant) are lower than for the ingredients used in black powder manufacturing; on the other hand, they would be greater than the major components of smokeless powder. The Microtrace (originally 3M) taggant has not been used in the manufacture of smokeless powder, but has been used in the manufacture of black blasting powder used in the Swiss mining industry for almost 20 years without incident.

Any of the four taggant categories could be produced in a form that does not require the addition of macroscopic particles akin to the Microtrace taggant. Examples range from biological materials that could be added at extremely low concentrations, to organic dyes, such as those that are now added to smokeless powders containing color-coded propellant granules to identify a particular product.

Although the addition of taggants at low concentrations and in nonparticulate form suggests that tagging may not affect the performance or safe handling of a powder throughout its manufacture and use, any new material proposed for use as a taggant in either black or smokeless powder would have to be carefully evaluated.

Wide Forensic Applicability and Utility for Law Enforcement

To some extent the law enforcement value of a taggant is directly related to its information content (Box 3.2). At one extreme, a taggant with high information content may be correlated with an individual package of powder, and recovery of a taggant at a crime scene could enable investigators to establish (through an audit trail through the sales and distribution network) a direct link with a bomber—or at least to the individual who purchased the powder. At the other extreme, a low-information taggant (such as the red propellant granules added to Alliant's Red Dot powder) might establish only the identity of the manufacturer and type of powder. But even here the value to law enforcement could be substantial. The existence of an audit trail could allow investigators to focus on the subset of sales of that particular type of powder, enabling them to enhance their traditional investigatory procedures in their search for possible suspects. Also, information about the purchase of a particular type of powder by a suspect might help law enforcement officials to establish sufficient probable cause and obtain a search warrant.

Even in the complete absence of any information from an audit trail, a taggant could provide useful information in a criminal prosecution. If a taggant recovered from the scene of a bombing or attempted bombing were found to be the same as that in black or smokeless powder found in the possession of a suspect, that information would be another piece of circumstantial evidence linking the suspect to the crime.

BOX 3.2 How a Taggant Can Assist Law Enforcement

There are various ways in which a taggant could be used by law enforcement personnel in identifying a bombing perpetrator or convicting a known suspect. The examples below are not meant to represent a complete list of uses; they instead provide illustrations of varied taggant applications.

Furnish Information That May Justify Issuance of a Search Warrant

Scenario 1. Unconsumed smokeless powder recovered at a bombing scene has been identified as to manufacturer and product type. During the past year, the manufacturer and its master distributor sold thousands of pounds of this product to eight retail outlets in the geographical area of the blast. These outlets also carry many other powder products. When an investigator shows a salesclerk at one of these outlets a number of photographs, including photographs of an individual under suspicion because of a possible motive, the salesclerk states that this individual has bought smokeless powder in the past, but the clerk has no idea what kind of powder was bought. On the basis of this information, a law enforcement agent would probably not be able to obtain a warrant authorizing a search of the suspected individual's premises.

Scenario 2. The unconsumed smokeless powder recovered at the bombing scene from Scenario 1 also contained a taggant that identifies the manufacturer, product, and date of manufacture. Records indicate that 100 pounds of the tagged product were sold to two retail stores in the geographic area of the blast. When investigators check the retail stores' records, they find that three individuals bought cans of the tagged powder. One of these individuals, who has a possible motive, signed the store's register when buying a 1-pound can of the tagged product 2 weeks before the blast. Under these circumstances, a magistrate might find sufficient "probable cause" to issue a warrant for the search of the purchaser's premises. The search might yield incriminating physical evidence, such as other materials used in making the bomb, which would not otherwise be found.

Furnish Information That May Lead to an Indictment

Scenario 3. During the legal search of the home of a suspect in a recent bombing, law enforcement agents find the remnants of a box of black powder that contains a taggant. The tagged powder matches the powder and taggant recovered after a previous pipe bomb incident for which no arrests have ever been made. This evidence could lead to an indictment of the suspect for the earlier bombing.

Constitute Evidence at Trial That May Lead to a Conviction

Scenario 4. No unconsumed powder was found at the scene of a bombing, but taggants were found at the scene. When the taggant code was determined, investigators concluded that the bomb had been filled with black powder manufactured by company X during a particular period. During a legal search of the home of a bombing suspect, law enforcement agents find remnants of black powder containing taggants that match those found at the bombing scene. The evidence of the match could be admissible at trial as it increases the probability that the suspect manufactured the bomb in question.

Chemical and Physical Compatibility with Black and Smokeless Powders

This characteristic refers to the compatibility of the taggant with the manufacturing process for black and smokeless powders as well as its compatibility with criteria for safety and performance of the final products. The issues and problems are similar to those discussed above for health and safety risks. For the U.S. Office of Technology Assessment (OTA) report (OTA, 1980), some testing was performed on the compatibility of the 3M (Minnesota Mining and Manufacturing Company) taggant with various black and smokeless powders (see Box 3.3 for excerpts from this report). Because follow-up testing has not been carried out since the moratorium on taggant research in the early 1980s,[17] there is no comprehensive information about the overall compatibility of this or any other taggant type with all black and smokeless powders.

Consequently, even in the absence of any predictable chemical interactions between a proposed taggant and a black or smokeless powder, one could not be certain that the two would be compatible. Any new material proposed for use as a taggant in either black or smokeless powder would have to be carefully evaluated for chemical and physical compatibility. (For further discussion on the types of tests necessary for investigating chemical and physical compatibility, and for a representative listing of organizations capable of conducting such tests, see Appendix G.)

Compatibility of Taggants in the Black Powder Process. The chemical and physical compatibility of black powder with many of the taggants now commercially available needs to be researched. Some questions to be addressed are the following:

• What reactions, if any, occur between the taggant material and the potassium or sodium nitrate, sulfur, and charcoal in black powder?
• If a reaction occurs, what are the effects of elevated temperatures, pressures, and water concentration?
• Can the taggant serve as a catalyst for the decomposition of the black powder?
• How would any reactions affect stability, sensitivity, and the ballistic performance of the black powder?

---

[17]The Treasury, Postal Service and General Government Appropriation Bill, 1981 (Committee on Appropriations), Title I, p. 9: "After considering all the factors involved, particularly a Congressional Office of Technology Assessment report, the [House Committee on Appropriations] is concerned that the state of the art in explosives tagging technology is not sufficiently advanced to warrant either implementation or further research and development of this particular program at this time." The committee is not aware of any federally funded research on taggants in explosive materials that has occurred since this appropriations report.

BOX 3.3   Selections from the 1980 Office of Technology Assessment (OTA) Report *Taggants in Explosives*

As noted earlier, research on integrating taggants into smokeless and black powder is highly limited. The analysis done by OTA covered addition of the (then) 3M taggant into both high and low explosives, and was based on independent research by the Aerospace Corporation (which received information from four subcontractors, Atlas, DuPont, Hercules, and Independent) (OTA, 1980; Aerospace, 1980). The OTA findings relating to smokeless and black powder were as follows:

• "Assuming, for purposes of analysis, that stability questions are successfully resolved and that technical development is successfully completed, both identification taggants and detection taggants would be useful law enforcement tools against most terrorist and other criminal bombers. Their utility against certain types of bombers would probably be quite high; their utility against the most sophisticated of terrorists and professional criminals is open to question." (p. 15)

• "The tests so far conducted create a presumption that there are no incompatibilities between the 3M identification taggant and dynamites, slurries, gels, emulsions, or black powder. Nevertheless, a fullscale qualification program is necessary before taggants can be added to all such materials." (p. 18)

• "The Aerospace Corp. takes the view that the compatibility tests with dynamites, gels, slurries, emulsions, and black powder generally are sufficient to permit implementation of a program to tag these substances." (p. 19)

• "No tests have shown increased explosive sensitivity due to the addition of the baseline 3M taggant (either encapsulated or unencapsulated). Similarly, no changes in electrical, general mechanical, or toxicity characteristics have been noted. Decreased chemical stability was noted, however, for one type of smokeless powder (Herco 22); decreased stability was also noted in one type of booster material (Composition B). The tests conducted to date clearly show that some chemical reaction takes place when Herco powder or Composition B is mixed with a high concentration of 3M taggants and then heated to a high temperature; further research is required to determine the nature and cause of the reaction. . . ." (p. 91)

• "At the present time, there appears to be an incompatibility between the 3M taggants and the Herco smokeless powder. Hercules has indicated that it does not consider the combination safe and has stopped all work on it. OTA feels that, on the basis of the tests just described, the conclusion must be drawn that the 3M taggants cannot be safely added to the Herco powder unless the present incompatibility is resolved. Some justification exists for questioning the validity of tests using severely increased concentrations of the taggant materials (50 percent in the tests v. 0.05 percent of encapsulated material in the proposed taggant program), but it has not been demonstrated that there is a threshold concentration below which the problem disappears, and that such a threshold would never be exceeded in practice." (p. 95)

• "Tests, similar to those conducted with Herco, were conducted with other smokeless powders; no loss in stability was noted for other Hercules powders, or for the Olin or Du Pont smokeless powders. The reaction, therefore, probably is between the melamine/alkyd and one of the sensitizers or stabilizers of the Herco. . . ." (p. 96)

• Can the reaction of a taggant with black powder be suppressed or eliminated without adversely affecting the desirable taggant characteristics and the performance of the black powder?

• Regarding biochemical taggants, are the biological materials capable of surviving in the sulfur-rich environment of conventional black powder?

Compatibility of Taggants in the Smokeless Powder Process. Similar concerns and a lack of information on the chemical and physical compatibility of taggants with smokeless powders exist as they do for black powder. A typical smokeless powder will have 5 to 10 components. These multiple components create a potential for complex and possibly adverse chemistry to exist between a smokeless powder and a taggant material. Information is lacking on the effects of various taggants on the rheology, chemical stability, sensitivity, and ballistic performance of smokeless powders. Also, little is known concerning taggant survivability in the various powder manufacturing processes. Clearly, the chemical and physical compatibility of taggants with smokeless powders also needs to be thoroughly researched.

Effects on Performance. While the smokeless powder industry routinely uses colored dyes (for example, in the manufacture of products such as Alliant Red Dot powders), the dyed granules are themselves propellant powders. The dye has been demonstrated to have no effect on the ballistics or on other physical properties of the powder. It is critical that the effects on performance of any other type of new additive be rigorously investigated. Examples of the types of ballistics testing that would need to be conducted in order to quantify the effects of taggants on the performance of powder used in ammunition are discussed in Appendix G. Also listed in Appendix G are some laboratories that are capable of conducting such tests.

No Adverse Environmental Impact or Contamination

Many of the issues related to environmental impact are the same as those considered above with respect to health and safety in manufacture and end use. There is a shift in focus, however, from those who are directly exposed to those who may be affected in the longer term by residues from manufacturing or discarded powders or from residues that survive the intended use of the powder as a propellant. For both new and existing taggant technologies, the decomposition rates of the taggant in the environment must be determined, and research must be performed on the potential environmental impact.

Low Cost to Various Links in the Chain of Commerce

Introduction of new regulation into any manufacturing process almost always incurs new costs, at least initially. On the issue of introducing taggants into black and smokeless powders, the question of the cost of this program must be considered in light of the relatively low cost of the final product.[18] A tagging system that is excessively expensive may drive some of the powder manufacturers and distributors out of business. In the absence of even a pilot taggant program in the black and smokeless powder industry, costs are difficult to establish definitively. However, the expertise of the committee, combined with the large number of briefings by and visits to representatives from the powder manufacturing and distribution businesses, and the limited experience of tagging in Switzerland, make possible reasonable discussions of the factors affecting costs.

Factors Affecting the Cost of Taggant Materials. The cost for any given taggant is generally expected to correlate directly with its level of information content. The frequency with which the taggant is changed and how much of each version of the taggant is purchased also affect the price. A low-cost taggant whose code never changes incurs minimal cost (an example is the addition of dye to the propellant granules). As stated earlier, however, such a taggant provides only information as to the identity of the company that manufactured the powder and, perhaps, the product line. At the other extreme, an expensive taggant that contains a great deal of information and whose code must be changed daily would be expected to have high costs for the manufacturers of black or smokeless powder. Presumably, the costs of taggants also depend on how much of each particular taggant code was purchased; economies of scale could reduce the taggant purchasing cost. Another factor that would affect the price of the taggant material needed is the concentration of taggant in the powder.

There are many possible and plausible combinations of lot sizes, loading levels, and cost per pound for unique taggants, each yielding a specific added cost for the taggant per pound of powder. In Switzerland, where 3M-type taggants are added to commercial explosives, added costs for the taggant have been reported as $0.08 and $0.16 per pound of explosive, depending upon the mesh size of the taggant. (In Switzerland, the 3M taggant is added to commercial dynamite in concentrations of 0.025 percent.)[19]

---

[18]Consumers can purchase a 1-pound canister of black or smokeless powder for between $15 and $20 at a standard retail outlet. The cost per pound can be lower if the quantity purchased is large (e.g., a 20-pound keg) or if the purchase is made through a gun club.

[19]Microtrace has stated that, depending on mesh size, the concentration of taggant could be much lower. Estimates are on the order of 11.5 ppm for 50-mesh taggant down to 0.72 ppm for 200-mesh taggant. This in turn would influence the overall cost. Although the 200-mesh taggant is much more expensive than the 50 mesh ($1,800 per pound versus $250 per pound), the weight of 200-mesh taggant required to have the same number of taggant particles per pound of black or smokeless powder is significantly less than for 50 mesh. As a result, the cost of using 200-mesh taggant per pound of powder is actually less than for 50-mesh taggant. Personal communication, William Kerns, Microtrace, Inc., May 12, 1998.

Estimates can be made of the expected order of magnitude of the cost of purchasing taggants to be added to black and smokeless powders. Table 3.2 gives a range of approximate costs for a variety of tagging schemes based on stated assumptions about taggant concentrations, the cost of the taggants per pound, the amount of powder produced annually, and the size of a powder lot. It is important to note that these cost estimates take into account only the cost of the taggant; attendant administrative, production, and processing costs to the smokeless or black powder manufacturer have not been estimated. Under these assumptions, the cost of taggants needed for a pound of powder remains relatively constant at between \$0.05 and \$0.50 for changing taggant codes for time intervals ranging from annually to daily. The costs go up if the added taggant is specific to each lot or shift.

Factors Affecting the Cost of Incorporating the Taggant. The cost of incorporating a taggant is dependent on how and where it is introduced in the manufacturing process. The two main parts of the production process that would be affected by tagging are the recycling of surplus powder and the cleaning out of the manufacturing equipment. As stated previously, in both black and smokeless powder production, a great deal of rework is involved, when powder from different stages of production is returned to the initial production step for various reasons. Contamination could result from the reworking of powder with old taggants already incorporated. The added costs to avoid such contamination would depend on where in the manufacturing process the taggant was added, the amount of reworking that occurred, and how often the taggant code was changed.

When the taggant code was changed, it would be necessary to clean out the production equipment completely to reduce the chances of contamination. The added costs of this cleaning would depend on the frequency of changing the taggant code, the difficulty involved in cleaning the equipment, the amount of production time lost, and the level of manpower required to clean out the equipment. Such costs could be significant. However, a low-information taggant that was rarely, if ever, changed would not be expected to incur high additional cost.

At least initially, additional cost would also be expected for new equipment to incorporate the taggant into the powder and for modifications to existing equipment and production methods. These start-up costs should decrease as the taggant methodology is perfected.

In Switzerland, 3M-type taggants are incorporated into black powder used for blasting. According to two manufacturers of this powder, one taggant code is used in 15 metric tons of powder (roughly 4 months worth of production), and the tagging process has not resulted in major cost increases.[20] This is the only

---

[20] Personal communications from Poudrerie d'Aubonne, Aubonne, Switzerland, June 8, 1998, and Kemijiska Industrija Kamnik, Kamnik, Slovenia, June 16, 1998.

TABLE 3.2 Estimated Costs of Taggant Material Depending on Concentration and Frequency of Change

Frequency with Which Taggant Code Is Changed	Pounds of Powder Produced During One Tagging Cycle	Pounds of Taggant Material Required per Change	Cost ($) of Taggant Material per Change	Cost ($) of Taggant Material per Pound of Powder[a]
Annually	6,000,000	1500.0 - 3000.0	300,000 - 300M	0.050 - 0.500
Semiannually	3,000,000	750.0 - 1500.0	150,000 - 150M	0.050 - 0.500
Monthly	500,000	125.0 - 250.0	25,000 - 250,000	0.050 - 0.500
Weekly	120,000	30.0 - 60.0	6,000 - 60,000	0.050 - 0.500
Daily	24,000	6.0 - 12.0	1,200 - 12,000	0.050 - 0.500
Per lot	10,000	2.5 - 5.0	1,000 - 5,000	0.100 - 0.500
Per shift	8,000	2.0 - 4.0	1,000 - 5,000	0.125 - 0.625

NOTE: The following assumptions are made:

1. A production rate of 6 million pounds per year, 3 shifts per day, 5 days per week, and 50 weeks per year. Reductions in this rate would be expected to increase tagging costs.

2. A smokeless powder lot size of 10,000 pounds. Smaller lots would cost more because of the increased frequency of taggant change.

3. A taggant concentration between 0.025 percent to 0.050 percent. Tagging in Switzerland is done at the 0.025 percent level; both Swiss law enforcement personnel and the 1980 Office of Technology Assessment report (OTA, 1980) recommend a 0.05 percent concentration by weight.

4. A taggant cost ranging from $200 per pound to $1,000 per pound, both with a 5-pound minimum purchase per code.

[a]This column represents the cost of purchasing the taggant materials and excludes any costs associated with the powder manufacturing process.

example of the use of taggants in black or smokeless powder; data on the costs of other taggant technologies or other rates of code changes are not available.

Factors Affecting Costs in the Distribution System. At present, record keeping in the distribution system is mainly an in-house process at the manufacturing or distribution facility; in general, no records are maintained that link records throughout the distribution system. Two methods of additional record keeping potentially may be employed. The first would consist of the powder packagers maintaining records of lot shipments to retailers or other distributors. The level of difficulty in implementing such a system would be expected to depend on the volume of sales and the number of customers. If the record keeping were simply carried out at each stage of distribution, the advantages provided by good records, such as increased information for sales and marketing purposes, might actually outweigh any added costs.[21] Alternatively, a centralized record depository may be put in place to track shipment throughout the distribution system. Besides the likelihood that such a repository would be cumbersome and expensive to maintain, confidentiality issues would be a key concern for the packagers and distributors.

Record keeping at the retail level can also provide law enforcement personnel with the opportunity to identify the last legal purchaser of smokeless or black powder. Current record keeping varies widely with both retailer and state (see discussion earlier in this chapter on record keeping at the federal, state, and local level). A nationwide requirement that customers sign for the purchase of black and smokeless powders is one system that could aid law enforcement personnel in their investigation of bombing incidents. As stated previously, even in the absence of a tagging program, several forensic investigators contacted by the committee indicated that it would be useful in bombing investigations to be able to obtain from local retailers a list of individuals who had recently bought the type of powder used in the bombing.[22] As with increased record keeping at the distribution level, the question of where the records would be kept, whether with the retailer or in a centralized record-keeping location, must be determined. Another consideration at this level is the privacy of an individual who purchases black or smokeless powder for legal uses. However, there are already some situations today in which purchasers of potentially dangerous items are required to show identification. For example, the purchase of prescription medicine at a pharmacy is one consumer transaction that requires registration information at

---

[21]These factors are contributing to the increasing use of bar codes to track products in all areas of commerce.

[22] Personal communications during site visits to the ATF and the FBI, March 19, 1998. See also Appendix F.

the point of sale. In this case, the regulation is designed to control the distribution of potentially dangerous drugs and ensure that they are used under the supervision of a physician.

Factors Affecting Costs to the End User. Increased cost from any taggant program may eventually be passed on to the consumer. But in the absence of accurate cost estimates for the above categories, no definitive estimate of this price increase can be made. The estimates of the costs of the taggant materials made in Table 3.2 indicate that the added cost could be expected to be at least $0.05 to $0.50 per pound of powder, which corresponds to a price increase of at least 0.3 to 3 percent for a $15 1-pound canister of retail powder.

No Viable Countermeasures

Various types of taggants have differing degrees of vulnerability to countermeasures. For example, water solubility may allow for the removal of a taggant by washing smokeless powder. Visible taggants may be removed manually. Other types of taggants may degrade over time, compared with the long shelf life of black and smokeless powders (from 20 to 50 years). Some taggants, such as biological materials, can be expected to have much greater resistance to countermeasures; however, they would be correspondingly more difficult to isolate and evaluate for forensic purposes. As noted earlier, depending on the amount of taggant associated with an individual powder granule, the Class II taggants may be inherently more vulnerable to countermeasures—either through partial destruction of certain components of the taggant, or through blending of two samples having different mixtures of taggant codes.

Besides actively tampering with the taggant in black or smokeless powder, other options are available for circumventing the effects of taggants completely. Homemade black powder is relatively easy to make, although the quality tends to be substandard, and the manufacturing process is dangerous. Recipes for the manufacture of black powder are readily available on the Internet.[23] Another option is to obtain untagged black or smokeless powder through the black market. A final consideration is that if black or smokeless powder used for reloading is tagged, bombers may seek out other sources of explosive materials to be used in improvised bombs. As a result, pyrotechnics and homemade chemical mixtures could become a more common ingredient in these illegal devices.

---

[23]The topic of Internet use for potential bomb makers is discussed in Cannistraro and Bresett (1998).

Unique Information That Is Easy to Read

While the usefulness of a taggant is somewhat related to the amount of information it contains, even a low-information taggant can still be valuable. A low-information taggant, such as dyed powder granules in smokeless powder, can provide investigators only with the product manufacturer and product line. However, forensic experts have indicated that the presence of red or blue dots in smokeless powder is sometimes of considerable help in their work, because this information can eliminate hundreds of other possible types of smokeless powder.[24]

With more sophisticated types of taggants, a great deal of information that possibly would allow tracing to individual 1-pound canisters of powder may be retrieved from a single taggant. However, as useful as this information may prove to be, the analysis is much more complicated than for a simple dyed-powder-granule taggant. For example, the instrumentation required to read the information from a DNA taggant can cost up to $70,000.[25] Isotopic taggants also require analysis using expensive instruments. The information content must be weighed against the added complexity and cost of the analysis. One proposed method to lower the costs to forensic laboratories is to subcontract the analysis of postblast powder evidence to independent laboratories for taggant retrieval and decoding.[26]

EXPERIENCE WITH TAGGANTS IN EXPLOSIVES

The experience with taggants in black powder and high explosives in Switzerland provides some information on the utility and difficulties that might be expected in developing or implementing taggants for the U.S. black and smokeless powder markets.

Taggants in High Explosives

Commercial implementation of taggants in explosives is largely limited to one type: a plastic multilayered chip in which the sequence of colored layers provides the coded information. This taggant was originally made by 3M and is now manufactured by Microtrace, Inc., in the United States. This taggant was

---

[24]Similar information might also be incorporated into the powder morphology by introducing intentional tool marks to the individual propellant granules during the extrusion process. This method would not require that a foreign substance be introduced into the powder.

[25]Keith Stormo, Innovative Biosystems, Inc., presentation to the committee, March 6, 1998.

[26]For example, companies that use taggants from Isotag LLC currently have the taggant retrieval and decoding performed by the taggant producer.

tested extensively for use in explosives and, to a more limited extent, for use in propellants during the 1970s and has been used by the Swiss explosives industry since 1981.[27] Because there are more test data on the use of Microtrace taggants in explosives than any other type of taggant, the term "taggant" has come to be identified in the popular press with this type of multilayered plastic chip. There is, however, a wide array of taggant concepts in various stages of development (see Table 3.1 and Appendix D). In addition, the use of taggants in nonexplosive commercial applications may provide guidance for the use of taggants in smokeless and black powder.

Use of Taggants in Switzerland

Switzerland requires the use of taggants in all explosives, including black powder used for blasting purposes. However, because smokeless powder and black powder sold for shooting purposes are not tagged, there is little information from the Swiss experience that is directly applicable to the task of the committee. For example, only a single instance of a bombing with tagged black powder was reported between 1989 and 1994 (NRC, 1998, p. 204, Table F.1). Currently, two manufacturers produce the type of black powder used in Switzerland as a blasting agent: Poudrerie d'Aubonne and Kemijiska Industrija Kamnik. Both companies report that they incorporate 3M taggants into the manufactured black powder at the beginning of the mixing operation, at concentrations of 0.025 percent by weight (the process of manufacture is very similar to that described in Chapter 1 and employed at Goex, Inc.). Poudrerie d'Aubonne tags approximately 40 metric tons of black powder per year, changing the taggant code every 15 metric tons. The cost of the taggant material is 550 Swiss francs per kg ($395.68 per kg),[28] with no information given on increased costs due to processing or record keeping, though records were said to be kept in the same manner as normal production records. The company reports no deviation from standard industry practice, nor any difficulties added to the process due to taggant inclusion. There are no special considerations taken to separate rework from the process, nor is concern raised over potential taggant contamination during a code change. The Slovenian company tags roughly 25 tons per year. It reports an increase in production costs owing to its policy of burning rejected material rather than recycling it and contaminating the taggant code.[29]

---

[27]The OTA (1980) report recommended that further research be conducted on identification taggants. The Aerospace (1980) report stated, "Test results to date indicate that the 3M taggant, as used in the pilot test, is satisfactory in all respects except for ease of field decoding" (p. 8-2).

[28]At an exchange rate of 1.3900, as published in the *New York Times*, September 22, 1998.

[29]Personal communication and materials received from Poudrerie d'Aubonne, June 8, 1998, and Kemijiska Industrija Kamnik, Kamnik, Slovenia, June 16, 1998.

As implemented in Switzerland, the taggant carries information about the explosive manufacturer, the product type, and general information about the time of manufacture (for reasons of manufacturer convenience, taggant codes are only changed every 6 months). The Swiss police consider their tagging program to be a success, based on the data about their bombing investigations. Between 1989 and 1994, the total number of incidents in Switzerland using black powder was 61, of which only 1 incident involved tagged black powder (there were 7 incidents involving smokeless powder, which does not contain taggants) (NRC, 1998). While the small number of incidents using tagged versus untagged black powder may argue in favor of the effectiveness of taggants, only black powder used for blasting purposes is tagged in Switzerland. Black powder used for sport shooting is not tagged. Presumably, black powder used for sport would be easier to obtain than black powder used for blasting and may account for this discrepancy in numbers. In addition, the overall low number of incidents makes any generalizations about the effectiveness of taggants difficult. Despite the reported success of the taggant program in Switzerland, no other country has chosen to adopt taggants in its explosives industry.

Taggants in Black and Smokeless Powders

As noted earlier, black and smokeless powders designed for shooting applications are not tagged in Switzerland. In the United States, OTA reported that tests on the Microtrace (then 3M) taggant in black and smokeless powder raised compatibility issues with one type of smokeless powder, Herco (OTA, 1980). Some compatibility testing was conducted by Lawrence Livermore Laboratory at elevated temperatures (80 to 120 °C) and taggant concentrations (50 percent).[30] Further research was recommended by OTA, but because research funding on taggants was terminated in the United States in 1980,[31] the compatibility of these taggants with propellant powders has not been definitively assessed. The results of the early testing on taggant feasibility were discussed in the 1980 OTA report, selections from which are given in Box 3.3.

The information provided by the OTA's 1980 report indicates that, at least

---

[30]Elevated temperature and concentration tests are routinely used for military and other testing to simulate worst-case and longer-term effects (Hall and Holden, 1988).

[31]The Treasury, Postal Service and General Government Appropriation Bill, 1981 (Committee on Appropriations), Title I, p. 9: "After considering all the factors involved, particularly a Congressional Office of Technology Assessment report, the [House Committee on Appropriations] is concerned that the state of the art in explosives tagging technology is not sufficiently advanced to warrant either implementation or further research and development of this particular program at this time." The committee is not aware of any federally funded research on taggants in explosive materials that has occurred since this appropriations report.

for the 3M taggant, no incompatibilities were found with black powder, and only one negative result with the Herco smokeless powder. OTA did not perform any performance or safety tests, but instead relied on data from research done at the Aerospace Corporation and on information provided by powder manufacturers. Aerospace Corporation's 1980 report does not mention any incompatibilities between the 3M taggant and smokeless powders.[32]

Though not intended as such, some commercial smokeless powders in the United States do already incorporate a kind of taggant. Alliant Techsystems manufactures smokeless powders that contain propellant granules marked with dyes of various colors. These Red Dot, Green Dot, and Blue Dot products aid the reloader by providing a visual identification of the product in a reloading machine. However, these dyed products also have served another purpose: bomb investigators have indicated to the committee that recovery of the dyed powder granules at a bomb scene facilitates the identification of the powder used and aids the investigation.[33]

SUMMARY

Depending on the amount of information encoded in the taggant, the frequency with which the manufacturer changes the codes, and the extent of record keeping in the distribution system, tagging of black and smokeless powders could provide investigators with information on the manufacturer, specific product type, and chain of ownership. Taggants could also help to determine if different bombing incidents are connected, and once a suspect has been identified, taggants from a bomb scene could be matched with taggants found in the suspect's possession in order to assist in the prosecution.

DISCUSSION

The current capabilities of investigators and possible benefits of taggants for the investigation of bombings using black or smokeless powders are summarized in Tables 3.3 and 3.4. The current ability to use chemical and physical methods

---

[32]During the committee's open meetings (see Appendix E), several participants commented on the possible implications of an explosion at a Goex manufacturing site in East Camden, Arkansas, that occurred in July 1979. As noted in the ATF's *Progress Report: Study of Marking, Rendering Inert, and Licensing of Explosive Materials* (Department of the Treasury, 1997), "While Goex asserted that taggants in boosters which were being reworked caused the explosion, it has never been established that taggants were involved in, or the cause of, the explosion." The committee further notes that the Goex plant in question was manufacturing high explosives rather than smokeless or black powder.

[33]Personal communication during subcommittee site visit, Ron Kelley, Federal Bureau of Investigation, March 19, 1998.

TABLE 3.3 Level of Current Capability in Chemical and Physical Analysis in a Forensic Investigation and the Incremental Value of Taggants

Task	Capability with Current Forensic Methods (without Taggants)			Incremental Value of Taggants
	For Black Powder	For Black Powder Replicas	For Smokeless Powder	
Identification of powder material[a]				
Burned[b]	High—characteristic inorganic residue usually present[c]	Low to moderate—decomposition powders have characteristics similar to those of pyrotechnic compositions	Not identifiable—combustion products are gases	May be high if taggant survives and no residue is recovered
Unreacted	Readily identifiable	Readily identifiable	Readily identifiable	Low—information usually available without taggants
Identification of manufacturer of powder material				
Burned	Low—inorganic residues only	Low—inorganic residues only	Not identifiable—combustion products are gases	May be high if taggant survives
Unreacted	Moderate—unburned black powder from the one U.S. manufacturer and some foreign manufacturers can be differentiated	Moderate to high—relatively few manufacturers, and powders tend to contain characteristic additives	High—powder size, morphology, and composition point to manufacturer	Moderate for black powder and replicas; lower for smokeless powder as information is already available

Identification of product line/type (granulation or designation)			
Burned	Low—inorganic residues only	Low—inorganic residues only	Not identifiable—combustion products are gases	May be high if taggant survives
Unreacted	Moderate—mesh size provides some information	Moderate—mesh size and chemical composition can provide useful information	Moderate—can distinguish between ball, flake, and extruded; more difficult to differentiate within these categories	Moderate to high—could identify product types if not already known

aAbility of chemical analysis to distinguish between smokeless powder, black powder, and black powder substitutes.

bBurned powder refers to the products resulting from deflagration of a powder in an explosion and excludes traces of unburned powder. This is an unlikely scenario, especially for smokeless powder, since unreacted powder is recovered or no solid combustion products remain. Further assumptions are made that no residue would have been dissolved by water or destroyed by fire.

cAlthough inorganic ions found in burned black powder are common in the environment, their high concentration at a bomb scene would be characteristic of burned blacked powder.

SOURCE: Adapted from information received on site visits by the committee (see Appendix F), presentations of law enforcement and forensic personnel, and Bender (1998).

TABLE 3.4 Capability of Law Enforcement to Trace a Known Powder Used in an Improvised Explosive Device

Task	Current Capability	Capability with Adding Record Keeping Only	Capability with Adding Taggants Only	Capability with Adding Taggants and Record Keeping
Identify a lot or batch	Low	Low	Low	High
Identify distribution chain	Low	Low	Low	High
Identify last legal purchaser	Low (moderate in significant cases where a large effort is made to investigate retail outlets)	Moderate—depends on the volume of sales of the powder	Low	High
Trace the powder in a bomb to possible suspects	Low (moderate in significant cases where a large effort is made to investigate retail outlets)	Moderate—effective if bomber is the last legal purchaser, no aid otherwise	Low	Moderate
Obtain supporting evidence[a]	Low to moderate—value depends on frequency of specific powder use	Moderate—could aid in identifying the time of powder purchase with respect to time of bombing	Moderate to high—value depends on frequency of taggant code change	High—record keeping may not be necessary if taggant code is sufficiently specific

[a]Represents the utility of record keeping and/or taggants in strengthening evidence linking powder in a known suspect's possession with that used in a bomb.

to identify black or smokeless powder is compared with the incremental value of adding taggants in Table 3.3. In Table 3.4, the incremental value of taggants is indicated in light of the increased ability to trace a particular powder from the manufacturer to the last legal purchaser.

Implications of Taggant Use for the Analysis of Black and Smokeless Powders

The incorporation of taggants in black and smokeless powders could affect the standard analytical procedures currently used by forensic scientists. An established minimum amount of taggant would have to be found to allow scientists to be sure that the presence of the taggant was not a result of some kind of contamination (at the manufacturing, environmental, or evidence-collection stages). This minimum amount would depend on the taggant type, the amount of taggant per pound of powder, and the frequency with which the taggant was changed. For example, in the case of the multilayer acrylic particle (Microtrace) taggant, the Aerospace report (1980) established that 20 particles should be found at the bomb scene to ensure statistical accuracy of their presence. In Switzerland, law enforcement personnel must find 10 like-coded taggants in order to declare the use of a tagged explosive material in the exploded device (Schärer, 1996). In U.S. courts, it is highly probable that conventional analysis would be required to supplement taggant-based evidence and to negate arguments about contamination.

If visible taggants were used, a microscopic analysis might suffice to identify the taggant's presence and decode its information without resorting to detailed chemical analysis. If a taggant were used that was too small to be seen, the microscopic examination of debris and dirt would have to proceed as it would in the absence of taggant analysis to ensure the recovery of significant items of evidence. The search for and analysis of small (molecular-level) taggants could then probably proceed using one of the methods currently employed in the identification and analysis of untagged black and smokeless powders.

Table 3.3 indicates what are believed to be the levels of success of current forensic techniques in addressing the different aspects of an investigation of powder used in an improvised explosive device, as well as the committee's judgment about the incremental potential of taggants to increase this capability. Unfortunately, neither the ATF nor the FBI maintain statistics on the solve rate of criminal bombings, and so it is difficult to evaluate quantitatively the potential of taggants to increase the solve rate. Swiss authorities have claimed that in cases where taggants are recovered at the scene of a bombing, the solve rate is higher than in cases where no taggants are recovered.[34]

---

[34]The solve rate in cases where taggants have been found was 44.4 percent, compared to 16.2 percent when no taggants were found (NRC, 1998). The committee notes that factors other than the presence of taggants have influenced these statistics.

Matching the Bomb Filler to Materials in a Suspect's Possession

As noted earlier, many items of physical evidence, including unconsumed powders, containers, batteries, timing devices, tape, and so forth, typically survive a bomb blast. These may be used by investigators to connect a series of incidents or help identify the perpetrator if they can be matched to similar items proven to have been acquired by a suspect or matched to items found in the suspect's possession. This latter match is possible only if a suspect has already been identified and a search warrant obtained.

Taggants recovered at the bombing scene would provide an additional piece of evidence that could help connect serial bombings or provide a match with similar taggants in powders in the suspect's possession. The more specific the taggant, the greater its utility for these purposes. As noted in Table 3.3, using taggants to match bomb filler material to materials in a suspect's possession, unlike tracing a particular powder through the manufacturing and distribution process, is independent of additional record keeping.

The data in Tables 3.3 and 3.4 indicate that current methods and techniques of forensic analysis of unburned smokeless powder or black powder residues recovered at the scene can be very helpful in determining the filler type, manufacturer, and even the product type, especially for smokeless powders. However, such recovered powders are by themselves of little value in identifying the last legal owner of the powder or in connecting the bomb to a particular suspect. Correspondingly, the incremental value of taggants is moderate for identifying the manufacturer and product type. The incremental value is relatively high for establishing the chain of possession of the powder if a record-keeping system is instituted with the taggant system, and the increase in the ability to link a particular bomb to a particular suspect is also high with either a record-keeping system or by using a sufficiently specific taggant code.

While Tables 3.3 and 3.4 indicate that taggants could have law enforcement benefits, at least in certain cases, there is a lack of data on both the costs and benefits of a tagging program that make a quantitative analysis impossible in the absence of further research. On the cost side, there is inadequate information to assess such factors as compatibility, health and safety impacts, and increased costs to manufacturers. On the benefit side, there are no data on current solve rates. Such information about the success rate of investigators in the absence of taggants would provide a baseline for judging the potential incremental value of taggants.

FINDINGS AND RECOMMENDATIONS

The first priority for law enforcement regarding explosive devices is to protect the public by implementing technology that assists in the detection of such devices, thereby preventing bombings and the resulting deaths, injuries, and property damage. However, once a bombing takes place, the identification and arrest of a suspect and the successful, efficient prosecution and conviction of the perpetrator become of paramount importance. The rapid apprehension and conviction of individuals responsible for bombings have three potential benefits: (1) once captured and convicted, individuals cannot repeat their crimes, (2) their arrest may deter others from trying similar activities, and (3) the public is reassured that order is maintained in the community.

Finding: More than 90 percent of the deaths and 80 percent of the injuries caused by pipe bombs that use black and smokeless powders occur in locations where security screening is not typically present.[35] The lack of a viable detection system to screen for or locate explosive devices in these areas underscores the need for technologies that can assist law enforcement personnel in effectively investigating bombing incidents and prosecuting the offenders.

Finding: The evidence that forensic investigators often recover at a bomb scene— such as unburned powder from smokeless powder bombs and characteristic residues or unburned powder from black powder devices—can enable identification of the powder manufacturer and product line, thereby assisting in investigation and prosecution.

When bomb technicians are examining the evidence from the scene of the crime, all residues and recovered fragments of components from the explosive device are closely scrutinized, because the identification of suspects and the conviction of guilty parties depend on a collection of many types of evidence. Information about the powder is an important component of the evidence. If a suspect is found to own or have purchased the type of powder used in a bomb, that information can be coupled with the suspect's possession of other components used to make the device (the same type of duct tape, wire, piping, and the like) to assist in arrest and prosecution. Therefore, the more detailed the information about the powder used, the more valuable it is as evidence. For smokeless powders, such unreacted powder is almost always found after an explosion, while unreacted black powder and black powder substitutes are recovered somewhat less frequently.[36] Currently, forensic scientists study the physical characteristics and chemical composition of unreacted black or smokeless powder found at a bomb scene in order to ascertain if the manufacturer of the powder or the product line can be determined. For black powder, this sort of information is usually

---

[35]See Table 1.4 in Chapter 1 for more information on black and smokeless powder bombings by target.

[36]Especially for smokeless powders, the container used in powder-based improvised explosive devices often ruptures before all of the powder has been consumed, and unburned powder is therefore spread among the blast debris.

dependent on the morphology and dimensions of the powder granules, and therefore it is more difficult to determine the specific manufacturer and product type from a small or damaged powder sample. For smokeless powders, information is often obtained from both the chemical composition and the morphology. Consequently, the manufacturer is more readily established, and it is frequently possible to identify the specific product type. Currently, the FBI and the ATF have powder databases containing complementary information about the physical characteristics and chemical composition of commercial smokeless powders to assist in identifying the manufacturer and product line. In addition, these agencies keep samples and/or information about the physical dimensions of various commercially available black powders.

Finding: *The existing databases of information about black and smokeless powders, although used extensively in bombing investigations, are incomplete.* As of early 1998, the powder databases contained information on a significant fraction of the powders commercially available in the United States, but no systematic approach has been taken to developing a comprehensive powder database or to maintaining and updating the current information. In investigations, forensic scientists do encounter smokeless and black powder samples that cannot be matched to samples in their powder databases.

RECOMMENDED ACTION: A comprehensive national powder database containing information about the physical characteristics and chemical composition of commercially available black and smokeless powders should be developed and maintained. Such a database would assist investigators in identifying the manufacturer and product line of these powders used in improvised explosive devices.

The ATF and the FBI share information contained in their powder databases. A joint database could provide a more efficient and effective tool for law enforcement.[37] Such an effort would also be strengthened by a formal program of cooperation with the powder manufacturers to systematically collect product samples and gather official information about chemical composition and analytic protocols. An informal relationship already exists between the manufacturers and the forensic community in which the manufacturers' assistance is readily obtained during investigations of specific samples.

Finding: *The minimal record keeping currently associated with the sale and distribution of black and smokeless powders does not allow tracing of a specific lot of powder from the manufacturer to the final retailer. At the retail level, there*

---

[37]In addition, access to an easily searchable, comprehensive database could provide valuable assistance to state and local forensic investigators.

is no uniform, comprehensive system for keeping records of sales of powders; current practices vary from state to state, and there are relatively few locales in which any registration occurs. In general, record keeping within the manufacturing facilities is comprehensive, but once a lot of powder has left the plant, it is not possible for the manufacturer to know where a given lot of powder is retailed. At the retail level, some state or local governmental regulations or store policies require the purchaser of black or smokeless powders to sign a register, which is kept by the retailer. Anecdotal evidence indicates that such registers have been used to assist law enforcement personnel in their investigations. However, the costs of such registration systems and the added benefit to law enforcement agents have not been thoroughly evaluated. Today, there are relatively few locales in which registration occurs. The potential value of record keeping is discussed further following the final recommendation of this chapter.

Finding: Taggants added to black and smokeless powder and/or an associated record-keeping system could assist a bombing investigation by (1) aiding in the identification of the powder, manufacturer, and product line; (2) aiding in tracing the chain of ownership of the powder to a list of the last legal purchasers; and (3) helping to match the powder used in a bomb to powder in a suspect's possession. A taggant's usefulness would depend on the kinds and amount of coded information it contained; the strength of the audit trail would depend directly on that information and the nature of the system for recording sales. Use of a taggant would require decisions about how much information would be encoded, how often the information would be updated or changed, and whether the taggant and record-keeping costs would outweigh potential benefits.

Finding: No tagging system has been fully tested to demonstrate its technical feasibility for use in all types of black and smokeless powders, although in some cases taggants have been added to powders for specific applications. The use of taggants in Switzerland for black powders intended for blasting, and the use of dyed powder grains in some smokeless powder products in the United States, indicate that some forms of taggants are technically feasible for some powder products. However, the suspension of federally funded research on taggants in explosives applications in the United States in 1981 has left many questions unanswered about the compatibility of taggants with the wide variety of black and smokeless powder products currently available.[38] Although new taggant

---

[38]The Treasury, Postal Service and General Government Appropriation Bill, 1981 (Committee on Appropriations), Title I, p. 9: "After considering all the factors involved, particularly a Congressional Office of Technology Assessment report, the [House Committee on Appropriations] is concerned that the state of the art in explosives tagging technology is not sufficiently advanced to warrant either implementation or further research and development of this particular program at this time." The committee is not aware of any federally funded research on taggants in explosive materials that has occurred since this appropriations report.

concepts have been proposed that may overcome some of the safety and compatibility concerns raised by the 3M-type taggant currently used in Switzerland, thorough studies have not been performed on the use of any of these proposed taggants in black and smokeless powders.

RECOMMENDATION: Identification taggants in black and smokeless powder should not be implemented at the present time.

Institution of a taggant program with its associated record-keeping system would incur significant costs. At the current threat level of fewer than 10 deaths and 100 injuries per year and very few terrorist incidents, the committee believes that benefits are not sufficient to justify a tagging program. If the threat increased substantially in the future, and test data were available, benefits might exceed costs, and a tagging program might be warranted.

A taggant program for black and smokeless powders would be justified only if three criteria were met: the frequency and severity of black and smokeless powder bombings were found to be high enough to justify tagging, the taggants first were thoroughly tested and found to be safe and effective under conditions likely to be encountered in the legal and illegal uses of the powders, and the benefits to society of taggants were found to outweigh the costs of their use. Since no tagging system has been fully tested to demonstrate its technical feasibility, it is not practicable to tag at this time.

RECOMMENDED ACTION: Research should be conducted to develop and test taggants that would be technically suitable for inclusion in black and smokeless powders should future circumstances warrant their use.

Although the committee believes that the current level of bombings using black and smokeless powders does not warrant the use of taggant technology, the situation could change for the worse in the future. If policymakers decide that the level and type of bombings require action to increase the tools available to help the investigators of bombing incidents, more needs to be known about what technologies would be helpful. Research needs to focus on discovering and testing taggant concepts in the context of the ideal taggant criteria described by the committee in Chapter 3 and in the context of the capabilities of the forensic community to identify untagged powders. The development and use of a comprehensive database of powder characteristics would help clarify the current scientific capabilities for the identification of untagged powders and focus attention on situations in which increased information from powder mixed with taggants would be helpful.

RECOMMENDATION: If the type or number of bombing incidents involving black and smokeless powders increases in a way that leads policymakers

to believe that current investigatory and prosecutorial capabilities must be supplemented, the committee recommends that use of taggants, additional record keeping, or a combination of both actions be considered, provided that the chosen taggant technology has satisfactorily met all of the appropriate technological criteria. Research on taggants, as recommended above, is therefore essential to develop options and demonstrate the technical viability of any taggant system that may be considered for implementation at a future date.

The response to an increased bombing threat would depend on the nature of these bombings and the state of the technologies available when the decisions were being made. The type of taggant program and/or level of record keeping could be chosen to reflect the threat that these measures were meant to counteract. Any tagging or record-keeping action considered would have to be evaluated in light of the costs and benefits associated with that particular option. Additionally, if legislation mandating tracking of powders through the retail distribution system were to be enacted, the potential for bombers to use powders from the military or from ammunition to circumvent the record-keeping system would have to be considered.

The use of taggants without an associated record-keeping system could help forensic scientists identify the manufacturer and product line of a powder from a bomb or it could be used to match powder recovered at the scene to powder in a suspect's residence or possession. Record keeping could be used in the absence of a taggant program to track a powder type through the distribution chain, which could give law enforcement personnel information about where the powder was sold, and registration of sales at the retail level could help build a list of purchasers in the area near the site of a bombing. The features of a combined taggant and record-keeping program would depend on the level of information in the taggant, the extent of the record keeping, and the degree of coordination between the two.

Both of the sample tagging and record-keeping schemes described above, as well as record keeping alone, would aid investigators in demonstrating probable cause in order to obtain a search warrant and access to a suspect's residence, vehicle, and so forth. All of the potential actions listed above would provide additional evidence that would assist in the prosecution of a perpetrator.

Bibliography

AB Bofors Nobelkrut. 1960. Manual on Powder and Explosives. Bofors, Sweden: AB Bofors.

Aerospace Corporation. 1980. Identification Tagging Pilot Test for Packaged, Cap-Sensitive Explosives: Final Report. ATR-80(5860-03)-1ND. Washington, D.C.: Aerospace Corporation.

Alcohol, Tobacco, and Firearms, Bureau of (ATF). 1994. Firearms State Laws and Published Ordinances, 20th Ed. Publication ATF P 5300.5. Washington, D.C.: Bureau of Alcohol, Tobacco, and Firearms.

Alcohol, Tobacco, and Firearms, Bureau of (ATF). 1997. 1995 Arson and Explosives Incidents Report. Publication ATF P 3320.4 (4/97). Washington, D.C.: Bureau of Alcohol, Tobacco, and Firearms.

Ball, A.M. 1961. Solid Propellants. U.S. Army Ordnance Engineering Design Handbook. ORDP 20-175, Explosives Series. Washington, D.C.: Office of the Chief of Ordnance.

Bender, Edward C. 1998. Analysis of low explosives. Chapter 11 in Forensic Investigation of Explosions, Alexander Beveridge, ed. London: Taylor & Francis.

Cannistraro, Vincent, and David C. Bresett. 1998. The Terrorist Threat in America. Arlington, Va.: The Chemical Manufacturers Association.

Code of Federal Regulations (Department of the Treasury, Bureau of Alcohol, Tobacco and Firearms 27 CFR, Parts 55 and 181, Recodification and Amendments to Explosive Materials Regulations [T.D.-ATF 87; Re: Notice Nos. 309 and 358] 46 FR 40382, August 7, 1981).

Conkling, John A. 1985. Chemistry of Pyrotechnics. New York: Marcel Dekker.

Cooper, Paul W., and Stanley R. Kurowski. 1996. Introduction to the Technology of Explosives. New York: Wiley-VCH.

Davis, Tenny L. 1943. The Chemistry of Powder and Explosives. New York: John Wiley & Sons.

DeForest, Peter R., R.E. Gaensslen, and Henry C. Lee. 1983. Forensic Science: An Introduction to Criminalistics. New York: McGraw-Hill.

Deppert, T.M., M.W. Barnes, I.V. Mendenhall, and R.D. Taylor (Morton Automotive Safety Products, Ogden, UT). 1994. Development of gas generants for passive automobile restraint systems. Paper presented at 2nd International Symposium on Sophisticated Car Occupant Safety Systems, November 29-30, Fraunhofer Institut fur Chemische Technologie, Karlsruhe, Germany.

Dugan, Regina. 1997. The Making of a Dog's Nose. Pp. 7-31 in Proceedings of NATO Advanced Research Workshop on Explosives Detection and Decontamination of the Environment, University of Pardubice, Zajickova 191, 53003 Pardubice, Czech Republic.

Elias, L. 1991. Vapor pressures of *o*-MNT, *p*-MNT, EGDN, and DMNB between -20°C and +50°C and solubility of DMNB in various solvents. AH-DE/5-WP/17. Paper presented at meeting of the International Civil Aviation Organization, Montreal, Quebec, Canada, September 23-27, 1991.

Federal Bureau of Investigation (FBI). 1995. Terrorism in the United States. Washington, D.C.: Federal Bureau of Investigation.

Federal Bureau of Investigation (FBI). 1997. 1995 Bombing Incidents. FBI Explosives Unit—Bomb Data Center, General Information Bulletin 97-1. Washington, D.C.: Federal Bureau of Investigation.

Federal Explosives Law. 1970. Pub. L. No. 91-452, 84 Stat. 952 (codified at 18 U.S.C. SS 841-848 [1955]).

Fung, Tony. 1985. Identification of two unusual pipe bomb fillers. Canadian Society of Forensic Science Journal 18(4):222-226.

Hall, Thomas N., and James R. Holden. 1988. Navy Explosives Handbook: Explosion Effects and Properties. Part III. Properties of Explosives and Explosive Compositions. Indian Head, Va.: Naval Surface Warfare Center, October.

Hodgdon Powder Company. 1995. Hodgdon Data Manual No. 26. Shawnee Mission, Kans.: Hodgdon.

Hoover, Reynold N. 1995. Learning from Oklahoma City: Federal and state explosives laws in the United States. Kansas Journal of Law and Public Policy (Fall):35-60.

International Civil Aviation Organization (ICAO). 1991. Convention on the Marking of Plastic Explosives for the Purpose of Detection. Document No. 9571. Montreal, Quebec, Canada: ICAO, March 1.

JASON. 1986. Blasting Cap Tagging Schemes. JSR-86-825. JASON Program/MITRE Corporation, Reston, Va.

JASON. 1987. Detection of Plastic Guns. JSR-87-825. JASON Program/MITRE Corporation, Reston, Va.

JASON. 1988. Detection of Liquid Explosives. JSR-88-850. JASON Program/MITRE Corporation, Reston, Va.

JASON. 1994. Tagging Explosives for Detection. JSR-89-750. JASON Program/MITRE Corporation, Reston, Va.

Jurman, S.E., and J.R. Gimler. 1966. High-temperature-resistant HMX propellant for PAD applications. Paper presented at 1st Interagency Chemical Rocket Propulsion Group/American Institute for Aeronautics and Astronautics Solid Propulsion Conference, June, Washington, D.C.

Kirk, Paul. 1974. Crime Investigation. 2nd Ed. Malabar, Fla.: Robert E. Kreiger.

Krauss, M. 1971. Explosives Detecting Dogs, Final Report. U.S. Department of the Army, U.S. Army Land Warfare Laboratory, Aberdeen Proving Ground, Md.

McVitty, Derek, and Robert Alan Hall. 1977. Investigation of bombs and explosives. In Forensic Medicine: A Study in Trauma and Environmental Hazard, Vol. I, C.G. Tedeschi, William G. Eckert, and Luke G. Tedeschi, eds. Philadelphia: W.B. Saunders.

Mohanty, Bibhu. 1998. Physics of explosion hazards. Chapter 2 in Forensic Investigation of Explosions, Alexander Beveridge, ed. London: Taylor & Francis.

National Fire Protection Association (NFPA). 1992. NFPA 921 Fire and Explosion Investigations: 1992 Ed. Quincy, Mass.: NFPA.

National Research Council (NRC). 1998. Containing the Threat from Illegal Bombings: An Integrated National Strategy for Marking, Tagging, Rendering Inert, and Licensing Explosives and Their Precursors. Washington, D.C.: National Academy Press.

National Shooting Sports Foundation. 1996. 1996 Hunting Participation and Attitude Survey. Prepared by Responsive Management, Harrisonburg, Va.

Office of Technology Assessment (OTA). 1980. Taggants in Explosives. Washington, D.C.: U.S. Government Printing Office.

Ramage, Kenneth C., ed. 1991. Lyman Reloading Handbook, 8th Ed. Middleton, Conn.: Lyman.

Rocchio, J.J., H.J. Reeves, and I.W. May. 1975. The Low Vulnerability Ammunition Concept—Initial Feasibility Studies. Ballistics Research Laboratory Memo Report BRL MR-2520. Aberdeen, Md.: U.S. Army Ballistics Research Laboratory, August.

Rouhi, Maureen A. 1997. Detecting illegal substances. Chemical and Engineering News, September 29, pp. 24-29.

Saferstein, Richard. 1998. Criminalistics: An Introduction to the Forensic Sciences. Upper Saddle River, N.J.: Prentice-Hall.

Schärer, Jürg. 1996. Switzerland's explosives identification program. Pp. 157-175 in Compendium of Papers of the International Explosives Symposium (preliminary proceedings of the International Explosives Symposium hosted by the Bureau of Alcohol, Tobacco, and Firearms, Sept. 18-22, 1995, in Fairfax, Va.). Washington D.C.: Bureau of Alcohol, Tobacco, and Firearms.

Schlesinger, Hank. 1998. Anticounterfeiting tags you can drink. Popular Science, July, p. 28.

Schubert, H., and H. Schmid. 1997. Future trends in gas generator systems. Paper presented at Challenges in Propellants and Combustion, 100 Years After Nobel, Stockholm, Sweden, May 1996. New York: Begell House.

Scott, Lee. 1994. Pipe and Fire Bomb Designs: A Guide for Police Bomb Technicians. Boulder, Colo.: Paladin Press.

Simmons, Ron L. 1964. Development of High-temperature-Resistant Propellants. Frankford Arsenal Report R-1703, RTD-TDR-63-4209, Contract DA-36-038-507-ORD-3572M, Hercules Powder Co., Kenvil, N.J., January.

Stoffel, Joseph. 1972. Explosives and Homemade Bombs. Springfield, Ill.: Charles C. Thomas.

Taylor, James. 1959. Solid Propellant and Exothermic Compositions. New York: Interscience Publishers.

Urbanski, Tadeusz. 1967. Chemistry and Technology of Explosives, Vol. III. New York: Pergamon Press, pp. 323-333.

U.S. Department of the Treasury. 1997. Canine Olfactory Sensitivity to a Selected Nitroglycerine-based Smokeless Powder. Prepared by Johnston, James M., and Hartell, Mark G., Institute of Biological Detection Systems, Auburn University, Auburn, Ala.

U.S. Department of the Treasury. 1998. Progress Report: Study of Marking, Rendering Inert, and Licensing of Explosive Materials. Washington, D.C.: Department of the Treasury.

Wallace, Cynthia L., and Charles R. Midkiff, Jr. 1993. Smokeless powder characterization: An investigative tool in pipe bombings. Pp. 29-39 in Advances in Analysis and Detection of Explosives, J. Yinon, ed. The Netherlands: Kluwer Academic Publishers.

White House Commission on Aviation Safety and Security, Vice President Al Gore, Chairman. 1997. Final Report to President Clinton. Washington, D.C., February 12.

Winchester Ammunition Company. 1996. Winchester Ammunition Product Guide 1996. East Alton, Ill.: Winchester/Olin Corp.

Wolfe, David, ed. 1991. Propellant Profiles, 3rd Ed. Prescott, Ariz.: Wolfe Publishing.

Yinon, Jehuda, and Shmuel Zitrin. 1993. Modern Methods and Applications in Analysis of Explosives. New York: John Wiley & Sons.

APPENDIXES

A

Biographical Sketches of Committee Members

Edwin P. Przybylowicz, chair, retired as senior vice president and director of research in 1991 after 36 years in research and development with Eastman Kodak Company. From 1994 to 1996 he was director of the Center for Imaging Science at the Rochester Institute of Technology. He has co-chaired the National Research Council's Board on Chemical Sciences and Technology and served on several NRC panels and committees. He is a member of the Board of Directors of the New York State Science and Technology Foundation and a commissioner on the U.S.-Polish Joint Commission for Cooperation in Science and Technology of the Department of State. He was elected to the National Academy of Engineering in 1990 and received the 1996 Malcolm Pruitt Award from the Council for Chemical Research.

Margaret A. Berger is the Suzanne J. and Norman Miles Professor of Law at Brooklyn Law School. She is an expert on the use of scientific evidence in criminal and civil judicial proceedings. She is the co-author of a multivolume treatise on federal evidence and several other books on evidence. She also contributed a chapter on "Evidentiary Framework" to the Federal Judicial Center's *Reference Manual on Scientific Evidence.* She has served as the reporter to the Advisory Committee on the Federal Rules of Evidence, as a consultant to the Carnegie Commission on Science and Technology, and as a member of the NRC Committee on DNA Technology in Forensic Science: An Update.

Alexander Beveridge is the head of the chemistry section of the Vancouver Forensic Laboratory of the Royal Canadian Mounted Police. He has had 30 years of forensic chemistry casework experience. His primary research interest is the analysis of residues from explosives, and he recently edited *Forensic Investigation of Explosions* (Taylor and Francis, London, 1998). Dr. Beveridge is a fellow of the Chemical Institute of Canada and a faculty member of the Open University of British Columbia. He earned his B.Sc. degree and Ph.D. in chemistry from Glasgow University, has an M.B.A. from the University of Alberta, and currently is studying law at the University of British Columbia. He was a member of the NRC Committee on Marking, Rendering Inert, and Licensing of Explosive Materials.

Leo R. Gizzi has over 25 years of experience in propellant manufacturing in the industrial community. He worked at Dupont before joining Hercules in 1972, where he worked mainly in propellant research and development as well as in quality management, becoming Quality and Technical Director at the Radford Army Ammunition Plant. His areas of expertise include propellant processing, quality control, ballistics, and chemical testing. Dr. Gizzi is knowledgeable about propellants for rockets, as well as for small-, medium-, and large-caliber guns used in commercial and military applications. He retired from Alliant Techsystems (previously Hercules, Inc.) in 1995. Currently Dr. Gizzi works as a freelance consultant specializing in propellants.

Janice M. Hiroms specializes in chemical management consulting. Her experience includes management of analytical services for ARCO Chemical Company and Lyondell Petrochemical Company as well as being vice-president for health, safety, and environment for Lyondell-Citgo Refining Company. She has a B.A. in chemistry and an M.B.A.

Karl V. Jacob founded the laboratory dedicated to solids processing at the Dow Chemical Company in 1989. The primary focus of his research has been on solids processing and particle and powder technology, specifically in powder mechanics and the drying and conveying of bulk solids. He is currently the vice-chair of the Particle Technology Forum, which is sponsored by the American Institute of Chemical Engineers.

Charles Parmenter is a chemical physicist and a professor who does experimental research on fundamental chemical reactivity and molecular energy transfer at Indiana University. He is a member of the National Academy of Sciences and the American Academy of Arts and Sciences. He is a fellow of the American Association for the Advancement of Science and the American Physical Society and has served on the editorial boards of several journals. He is currently on the NRC Office of Scientific and Engineering Personnel's Panel on Chemical Sciences and has also served on the Air Force Office of Scientific Research Chemical Sciences Review Panel.

Per-Anders Persson is a professor of mining engineering at New Mexico Institute of Mining and Technology, director of the Institute's Research Center for Energetic Materials, and chief scientist of its Energetic Materials Research and Testing Center, responsible for directing projects on safety and hazards of energetic materials. He is the inventor of the widely used NONEL fuse and detonator system and co-author of two textbooks, *Detonics of High Explosives*, with Johansson (Academic Press, San Diego, Calif., 1970) and *Rock Blasting and Explosives Engineering*, with Holmberg and Lee (CRC Press, Boca Raton, Fla., 1996). The recipient of a Ph.D. in physical chemistry from Cambridge University, England, and a former director of research and development for the Swedish explosives company Nitro Nobel AB, he has conducted studies in propellant and explosives burning, internal ballistics of guns, and the safety of energetic materials. He is a member of the Royal Swedish Academy of Engineering Sciences.

Walter F. Rowe is chair and professor of forensic sciences at the George Washington University. He is a physical chemist who focuses on chemical techniques that may be used in the course of criminal investigations. His current research includes work on the detection of smokeless powder residues from pipe bombs. He is a fellow of the Criminalistic Section of the American Academy of Forensic Sciences and a member of the editorial board of *The Journal of Forensic Sciences*.

Roger L. Schneider is a consultant in energetic materials with Rho Sigma Associates, Inc., specializing in pyrotechnics. His expertise includes chemical formulation, testing, analysis, and evaluation of energetic materials, as well as loss prevention. He serves frequently as an expert witness and has completed many accident reconstructions involving energetic materials. Since 1991, he has conducted research efforts for the U.S. Army Corps of Engineers' Construction Engineering Research Laboratories, Champaign, Illinois, developing environmentally benign technologies for the disposal of energetic material production waste. Naval Reserve Captain Schneider was assigned during his last 7 years of service to naval research activities until his retirement in March 1998. He had collaborated with energetic material research staff at the Office of Naval Research, Naval Surface Warfare Center-Indian Head and the Naval Research Laboratory. Schneider has a Ph.D. degree (University of Wisconsin-Milwaukee, 1982) in physical inorganic chemistry with minors in mechanical engineering and physics.

Ronald L. Simmons is a senior technologist/project manager with the U.S. Navy, with more than 40 years of experience with solid propellants for guns, rockets, and explosives, including smokeless powder for small-arms ammunition. Before coming to the naval facility at Indian Head, he worked for Hercules and Rocketdyne, commercial producers of propellants. He is an associate fellow of the American Institute of Astronautics and Aeronautics.

Judith Bannon Snow leads the High Explosives Science and Technology group at Los Alamos National Laboratory and is involved with explosives synthesis, formulation, chemical analysis, mechanical properties testing, micro-mechanical physics, nonshock initiation, deflagration to detonation theory, slow combustion, thermal studies, safety assessment, performance assessment, aging studies, and demilitarization of energetic materials. Prior to coming to Los Alamos, she spent 10 years at the Naval Undersea Warfare Center in New London, Connecticut, where she directed the Marine Optics Laboratory. Previously, she did nonlinear optics research in applied physics at Yale University. Dr. Snow has two patent awards and numerous scientific publications in laser spectroscopy, microparticle scattering, and nonlinear optics. She earned a Ph.D. in chemistry from Wesleyan University (Connecticut) and was a Sloan Fellow at the Stanford University Graduate School of Business, where she received an M.S. in management. She was a member of the NRC Committee on Marking, Rendering Inert, and Licensing of Explosive Materials.

Ronald R. Vandebeek is the laboratory manager for the Canadian Explosives Research Laboratory (CERL), Canada Centre for Mineral and Energy Technology. He works on testing, hazard evaluation, and development of energetic materials. He has been at CERL for 27 years and has been manager of the facility since 1981. The responsibilities of CERL include the technical issues related to classification and regulation of explosives, as well as environmental effects of their use.

Raymond S. Voorhees oversees the research and examination programs and activities of the Physical Evidence Section, U.S. Postal Inspection Service, which is responsible for nationwide crime scene response, including bombings. He also continues to work as a forensic analyst, performing chemical, instrumental, and microscopic examinations of physical evidence, and testifying about the results of such work. Before joining the U.S. Postal Inspection Service in 1983, he spent 13 years with the Metropolitan Police Department of Washington, D.C.

B

Statement of Task and Enabling Legislation

STATEMENT OF TASK

The following statement of task is reprinted from the contract between the Department of the Treasury's Bureau of Alcohol, Tobacco, and Firearms and the National Research Council.

The study required by this SOW [statement of work] should focus on matters of science and technology, with the goal of furnishing a report that provides a clear description of the technical issues that exist. The report should provide information that will facilitate decisions by the Secretary of the Treasury for recommendations to Congress.

TASK 1. Adding Tracer elements to black powder and smokeless powder for detection. The purpose of this task is to explore and define methods, materials and technologies that are available today, as well as those currently in research and development, that might be used to enhance the detectability of black powder or smokeless powder. In conducting this work step, the contractor shall determine whether:

SUBTASK 1.1. Tracer elements identified as candidates for use as detection agents will pose a risk to human life or safety.

SUBTASK 1.2. Tracer elements identified as candidates for use as detection agents will substantially assist law enforcement officers in their investigative efforts.

SUBTASK 1.3.   Tracer elements identified as candidates for use as detection agents will substantially impair the quality and performance of the powders (which shall include a broad and comprehensive sampling of all available powders) for their intended lawful use, including but not limited to the sporting, defense, and handloading uses of powders, as well as their use in display and lawful consumer pyrotechnics. At least three organizations that are capable of conducting testing to validate the study findings shall be identified.

SUBTASK 1.4.   Tracer elements identified as candidates for inclusion as detection agents will have a substantial adverse effect on the environment.

SUBTASK 1.5.   The addition of materials as tracer elements will incur costs which outweigh the benefits of their inclusion, including an evaluation of the probable production and regulatory cost of compliance to the industry and the costs and effects on consumers, including the effect on the demand for ammunition.

SUBTASK 1.6.   Tracer elements identified as candidates for inclusion can be evaded, and with what degree of difficulty, by terrorists or terrorist organizations, including evading tracer elements by the use of precursor chemicals to make black powder or smokeless powder.

TASK 2.   Adding Tracer elements to black powder or smokeless powder for identification. The purpose of this task is to explore and define methods, materials and technologies that are available today, as well as those currently in research and development, that might be used to identify the point of origination of black powder or smokeless powder. In conducting this work step, determine whether:

SUBTASK 2.1.   Tracer elements identified as candidates for inclusion as identification agents will pose a risk to human life or safety.

SUBTASK 2.2.   Tracer elements identified as candidates for inclusion as identification agents will substantially assist law enforcement officers in their investigative efforts.

SUBTASK 2.3.   Tracer elements identified as candidates for inclusion as identification agents will substantially impair the quality and performance of the powders (which shall include a broad and comprehensive sampling of all available powders) for their intended lawful use, including but not limited to the sporting, defense, and handloading uses of powders, as well as their use in display and lawful consumer pyrotechnics. At least three organizations that are capable of conducting testing to validate the study findings shall be identified.

SUBTASK 2.4. Tracer elements identified as candidates for inclusion as identification agents will have a substantial adverse effect on the environment.

SUBTASK 2.5. The addition of materials as tracer elements will incur costs which outweigh the benefits of their inclusion, including an evaluation of the probable production and regulatory cost of compliance to the industry and the cost and effects on consumers, including the effect on the demand for ammunition.

SUBTASK 2.6. Tracer elements identified as candidates for inclusion can be evaded, and with what degree of difficulty, by terrorists or terrorist organizations, including evading tracer elements by the use of precursor chemicals to make black powder or smokeless powder.

ENABLING LEGISLATION

In August 1996, the National Research Council contracted with the Treasury Department to carry out a study on the marking, rendering inert, and licensing of explosive materials. This study resulted directly from language in the Antiterrorism Act of 1996 (Public Law 104-132, Section 732). Smokeless and black powder were explicitly excluded from the study by subsection (a)(2) of the law.

In September 1996, the law was amended by the addition of a new subsection as follows:

(f) SPECIAL STUDY.—

(1) IN GENERAL.—Notwithstanding subsection (a), the Secretary of the Treasury shall enter into a contract with the National Academy of Sciences (referred to in this section as the "Academy") to conduct a study of the tagging of smokeless and black powder by any viable technology for purposes of detection and identification. The study shall be conducted by an independent panel of 5 experts appointed by the Academy.

(2) STUDY ELEMENTS.—The study conducted under this subsection shall-

(A) indicate whether the tracer elements, when added to smokeless and black powder-

(i) will pose a risk to human life or safety;

(ii) will substantially assist law enforcement officers in their investigative efforts;

(iii) will impair the quality and performance of the powders (which shall include a broad and comprehensive sampling of all available powders) for their intended lawful use, including, but not limited to the sporting, defense, and handloading uses of the powders, as well as their use in display and lawful consumer pyrotechnics;

(iv) will have a substantially adverse effect on the environment;

(v) will incur costs which outweigh the benefits of their inclusion, including an evaluation of the probable production and regulatory cost of compliance to the industry, and the costs and effects on consumers, including the effect on the demand for ammunition; and

(vi) can be evaded, and with what degree of difficulty, by terrorists or terrorist organizations, including evading tracer elements by the use of precursor chemicals to make black or other powders; and

(B) provide for consultation on the study with Federal, State, and local officials, non-governmental organizations, including all national police organizations, national sporting organizations, and national industry associations with expertise in this area and such other individuals as shall be deemed necessary.

(3) REPORT AND COSTS.-The study conducted under this subsection shall be presented to Congress 12 months after the enactment of this subsection and be made available to the public, including any data tapes or data used to form such recommendations. There are authorized to be appropriated such sums as may be necessary to carry out the study.

In October 1997, PL 105-61 111 Stat. 1272 extended the due date for the report as follows:

Provided, That section 113(2) of the Fiscal Year 1997 Department of Commerce, Justice, and State, the Judiciary, and Related Agencies Appropriations Act, Public Law 104-208 (110 Stat. 3009-22) is amended by striking "12 months" and inserting in lieu thereof "2 years."

C

Committee Meetings

The Committee on Smokeless and Black Powder held two information-gathering meetings during which it solicited presentations from various stakeholder groups, including law enforcement, powder user and manufacturer groups, taggant vendors, and detection experts. The committee also received written information from interested parties throughout its term of operation. In addition to holding open meetings, the committee made site visits to relevant manufacturers and law enforcement laboratories, as well as to a propellant distributor. Two meetings of the committee were devoted to analysis of information and writing of the final report.

First Meeting, January 14-16, 1998

Presentations

Charge to the Committee
  Hubert E. Wilson, Bureau of Alcohol, Tobacco, and Firearms, Washington, D.C.
Bombing Threat from Powder Devices
  Gregory A. Carl, Materials and Devices Unit, Explosives Group, Federal Bureau of Investigation, Washington, D.C.
Virginia Experience with Powder Bombings and Taggants
  Roger E. Broadbent, Virginia State Police
Security Protocols and Canine Detection of Smokeless Powder
  Anthony Cantu and John Hudson, U.S. Secret Service, Washington, D.C.
Muzzleloading and Black Powder
  John A. Miller, National Muzzleloading Rifle Association

Testimony on Taggants
  Tanya K. Metaksa, National Rifle Association, Fairfax, Va.
Arms and Ammunition Manufacturer Issues on Tagging and Detection
  James J. Baker, Donald Burton, and Kenneth D. Green, Sporting Arms and Ammunition Manufacturers Institute
State of the Art in Explosives Detection
  Lyle O. Malotky, Federal Aviation Administration, Washington, D.C.

Second Meeting, March 5-6, 1998

Presentations

Manufacturing of Black Powder
  Mick Fahringer, Goex, Inc., Doyline, La.
Manufacturing of Smokeless Powders
  Antonio Gonzalez, PRIMEX Technologies, St. Marks, Fla.
Inherent Taggants and Bomb Scene Investigations
  Richard A. Strobel, Bureau of Alcohol, Tobacco, and Firearms, Rockville, Md.
Air Bag, Cartridge-Actuated Devices/Propellant-Actuated Devices Technologies
  J. Scheld, U.S. Navy
History of Tagging
  Richard G. Livesay, 3M (retired), St. Paul, Minn.

Taggant Concepts:
Biocode, Inc.
  James Rittenburg, Biocode, Inc.
Caribbean Microparticles
  Abraham Schwartz, Caribbean Microparticles
Chemical Delivery Systems, Inc.
  Victor A. Crainich, Chemical Delivery Systems, Inc.
Innovative Biosystems, Inc.
  Keith Stormo, Innovative Biosystems, Inc.
Isotag LLC
  D. King Anderson, Isotag LLC
Materials Research Center, University of Missouri, Rolla
  Delbert E. Day, Materials Research Center, University of Missouri, Rolla
Mo-Sci Corp.
  Delbert E. Day, Materials Research Center, University of Missouri, Rolla
Microtrace, Inc.
  William J. Kerns, Microtrace, Inc.
Natura, Inc.
  Joel Dulebohn, Natura, Inc.

Tracer Detection Technology Corporation
   Jay Fraser, Tracer Detection Technology Corporation
Marking Proposal, Gadolinium-157
   Tim Hossain

Third Meeting, May 1-3, 1998

Committee Deliberations

Fourth Meeting, June 15-16, 1998

Committee Deliberations

Subcommittee Site Visits

March 4, 1998	Alliant Techsystems/New River Energetics
March 17, 1998	PRIMEX Technologies, Inc.
March 18, 1998	National Rifle Association Headquarters
March 19, 1998	Bureau of Alcohol, Tobacco, and Firearms National Laboratory Center
March 19, 1998	Federal Bureau of Investigation, Explosives and Chemistry Units
April 22, 1998	Goex, Inc.
May 22, 1998	Winchester Ammunition Plant
May 29, 1998	Hodgdon Powder Company

D

Taggant and Marker Concepts

To supplement its knowledge of current taggant and marker technologies, the Committee on Smokeless and Black Powder listened to brief presentations from a variety of vendors on March 6, 1998. The paragraphs below summarize the presentations to the committee.[1]

TAGGANT PRESENTATIONS

Biocode, Inc.

Biocode, Inc., uses a molecular binding pair technology; small organic chemicals are used as taggants, and code reading is accomplished by immunoassay. The material may by adsorbed to a substrate and may wash out in water. Material costs are estimated at pennies per unit, and applications to gasoline tagging are reported to be on the order of hundredths of a cent per gallon. The taggant could go in during manufacture or into the finished product. The technology has been used for clinical diagnostics and food and environmental testing. The technology has been employed in pharmaceutical, petrochemical, and agricultural industries.[2]

---

[1]In addition to the summaries listed in this appendix, the committee received written information on taggant concepts from CNC Development, Inc., February 2, 1998, and April 11, 1998; and Plexis BioSciences, LLP, May 7, 1998.

[2]James Rittenburg, Biocode, Inc., presentation to the committee, March 6, 1998.

Caribbean Microparticles

Caribbean Microparticles Corp. proposed the use of uniform polymeric microbeads (2-20 microns) for tagging powders (>1,000 microns). Individual populations of physically differing taggants could be mixed to provide a specific code. Dispersion of the microbeads would be best conducted in a liquid, but could be accomplished through dry mixing. These particles are hydrophobic and adhere to the powder particles so that washing, even with surfactants, does not remove them. Since identification of the specific populations is all that is required, only a representative sample of particles need be examined. Quantitative recovery of particles is not necessary. This technology is presently used in the tagging of documents and tracing of stamps, and has undergone survivability tests in shotgun blasts.[3]

Innovative Biosystems, Inc.

Innovative Biosystems, Inc., proposed addition of single-strand DNA, called Genetag™, to powders. DNA amplification would be accomplished through polymerase chain reaction (PCR) techniques. The genetic material was reported to survive temperatures of 60 °C for 1 year and to have been tested with powders through burning, simulated explosions, and shotgun blasts, with PCR amplification delivering readable codes. Company estimated costs are $500 to $1,000 for a 10k to 60k lb. batch with one taggant code, adding at the 7 ppm level. Cross-contamination and environmental persistence have not been fully studied.[4]

Isotag LLC

Isotag LLC proposed a mass enhanced molecular twin concept through isotopic substitution in explosive samples and identification with mass spectroscopy. Test explosions have been performed with 1 to 5 lb. tagged lots, and a 2,000 lb. lot of ammonium nitrate-fuel oil, tagged at ppb concentration, was exploded with reported postblast identification of codes. Analysis may be performed on dirt or debris samples. Studies have not been done using this technology with black powder. This technology has been used to tag lubricants, gasoline, and adhesives.[5]

---

[3]Abraham Schwartz, Caribbean Microparticles, presentation to the committee, March 6, 1998.
[4]Keith Stormo, Innovative Biosystems, Inc., presentation to the committee, March 6, 1998.
[5]D. King Anderson, Isotag LLC, presentation to the committee, March 6, 1998.

Materials Research Center and Mo-Sci Corporation

The Materials Research Center of University of Missouri-Rolla and Mo-Sci Corporation proposed the addition to powders of microscopic glass spheres encapsulating inert common and rare earth elements. Identification would be achieved through scanning-electron microscopy of surviving glass microspheres recovered from bomb residue. The technology has been tested on exploded pipe bombs and is reportedly stable to 3,000 °C. Varying-density solid or hollow spheres can be manufactured at reported prices of $0.10 to $0.20 per pound. These spheres have a greater hardness than that of potassium nitrate. The technology has been used as a radiation delivery system for treating human liver cancers.[6]

Microtrace, Inc.

Microtrace, Inc., presented the Microtaggant™ technology, a multilayered plastic particle. A code is created by altering the order of colors in the layers. The original technology (and associated patent) was developed by 3M in the 1970s, and has been in use in explosives (including black powder for blasting purposes) in Switzerland since 1980, as well as in other U.S. products for nonexplosive purposes. The Microtaggant™ was analyzed by the Office of Technology Assessment and Aerospace Corporation studies of 1980 (see Chapters 1 and 3). Enhancements by Dow and Eastman have reportedly increased the original code capacity 400 times.[7]

MARKER PRESENTATIONS

The following technologies were proposed to the committee to aid in the preblast detection of smokeless and black powder.

Chemical Delivery Systems, Inc.

Chemical Delivery Systems, Inc., proposed use of encapsulated frangible particles and masked detection materials as both a detection marker and identification taggant. The encapsulated samples are volatile and may be detected through odor, the specific molecule encapsulated, or by canine pheromones. Predicted cost for black and smokeless powder development was $500,000. No compatibility studies have been performed with black and smokeless powders. The technol-

---

[6]Delbert E. Day, Materials Research Center and Mo-Sci Corporation, presentation to the committee, March 6, 1998.

[7]William Kerns, Microtrace, Inc., presentation to the committee, March 6, 1998.

ogy is used commercially in sleep aids, toothpaste, and antiperspirants, and by the U.S. Army for crowd control.[8]

Natura, Inc.

Natura, Inc., proposed using "Luminate" technology, a mixture of amino acids, metal oxides, and organic acids that are chemically attached to powders as a marking system. It is reportedly available as a water soluble or insoluble solid, liquid, or cream, and is stable to 250 °C. Detection would target luminescence or encapsulated odors. Incorporation costs are predicted to be on the order of pennies per pound. Approximately 20 companies are testing this technology, including pharmaceutical, paper and ink, and glue companies. The technology is reported to have an unlimited shelf life.[9]

Tracer Detection Technology Corporation

Tracer Detection Technology Corporation proposes the addition of vapor-emitting encapsulated perfluorocarbons to powders for detection and identification at the ppb level. Identification is made by use of gas chromatography equipped with an electron capture detector. There are seven compounds with a range of fingerprints. Perfluoromethyl and dimethyl cyclohexane may be used with no change in sensitivity. The microcapsule responds to external stimuli. Detection occurs in an electron capture detector. A microcantilever solid state sensor is used. The system is turnkey, with detection possible from a range of one yard. The technology has been tested on black powder with inconclusive results.[10]

Tim Z. Hossain (Gadolinium-157)

The use of gadolinium or a gadolinium-157 taggant was proposed for powder detection, using prompt gamma detection following excitation of the particles. This tag may be incorporated into microparticles. The proposed isotope has a large capture cross section, improving the signal-to-noise ratio, although the cost of marker addition is unresolved. The isotopes are stable, and the excitation probe as well as the prompt gamma emissions are reportedly sufficiently penetrating to detect materials concealed in high-density containers such as steel casings.[11]

---

[8]Victor Crainich, Chemical Delivery Systems, Inc., presentation to the committee, March 6, 1998.

[9]Joel Dulebohn, Natura, Inc., presentation to the committee, March 6, 1998.

[10]Jay Fraser, Tracer Detection Technology Corporation, presentation to the committee, March 6, 1998.

[11]Tim Hossain, presentation to the committee, March 6, 1998.

ADDITIONAL CONCEPTS

In addition to the taggant presentations heard by the Committee on Smokeless and Black Powder, materials and presentations received by the NRC Committee on Marking, Rendering Inert, and Licensing of Explosives Materials were also reviewed. Presentations made to that committee are summarized below.

BioTraces, Inc.

BioTraces, Inc., principally makes instrumentation for detection and quantification of low levels of biomolecules. Company representatives proposed a taggant concept based on the use of multiphoton detection of appropriate biological and organic molecules.[12]

Cambridge Isotope Laboratories, Inc.

Cambridge Isotope Laboratories, Inc., synthesizes molecules (including some explosive compounds) tagged with stable, nonradioactive heavy isotopes. These isotopes are used mainly for biochemical and environmental trace analysis. Tagging of explosives through use of this approach was proposed.[13]

Centrus Plasma Technologies, Inc.

In written testimony,[14] Centrus Plasma Technologies, Inc., proposed using small quantities of enriched, stable isotopes (either as bonded isotopes in a compound or as a fine powder added to an explosive)—detectable by mass spectrometry—to tag explosives. According to Centrus, the use of an admixture has the advantages of avoiding complete dispersal in a detonation of high-grade explosive and of being a clear indicator for the included tag. The small quantities of isotopes required and the fine powder admixtures are believed to minimize any adverse effects on the tagged explosive materials. Projected industry costs for this method were estimated by Centrus to be in the range of $40 million to $60 million per year.

---

[12]Andrzej Drukier and James Wadiak, BioTraces, Inc., presentation to the NRC Committee on Marking, Rendering Inert, and Licensing of Explosive Materials, January 14, 1997, and information from BioTraces, Inc.

[13]Daniel Bolt, Cambridge Isotope Laboratories, Inc., presentation to the NRC Committee on Marking, Rendering Inert, and Licensing of Explosive Materials, January 14, 1997, and information from Cambridge Isotope Laboratories, Inc.

[14]Bruce Freeman, Centrus Plasma Technologies, Inc., "Explosive Tagging with Stable Isotopes," 1996.

MICOT Corporation

In written testimony,[15] MICOT Corporation proposed using a taggant consisting of randomly shaped particles made from a chemically stable thermoplastic resin, encoded with a custom numerical code combination of 10 or more colored layers. MICOT™ particles are detectable with an ultraviolet lamp or magnet and come in sizes from 15 to 1,000 microns (or higher). The availability of particle sizes ranging from 5 to 8 microns with five colored layers is projected for 1998.

Micro Dot Security Systems, Inc.

In written testimony,[16] Micro Dot Security Systems, Inc., proposed a self-contained, small, precision-cut polyester disk to mark or identify explosives. The Micro•Dot® can be coded with a variety of substrates, such as ultraviolet ink that fluoresces under black light for easy detection. It is imprinted with a 9- to 12-digit number that is a unique, one-of-a-kind sequence selected by the buyer.

Micro Tracers, Inc.

Micro Tracers, Inc., produces Microtracers™—colored, uniformly sized particles of iron grit, iron alloy, graphite, stainless steel, or silica gel that are analyzed through colorimetric techniques—that currently are used in animal and poultry feed and in building materials.[17] They have been used in more than 300 million tons of animal and poultry feed since the 1960s at a reported cost of $0.10 per ton. The company has only limited experience in explosives mixing operations, although it believes that its general approach could be adaptable to explosives applications.

Science Applications International Corporation

In written testimony,[18] Science Applications International Corporation proposed a detonator detection system based on multiphoton detection, a technique based on measurement of radioisotopic tracers whose decay is accompanied by

---

[15]Klaus Zimmermann, MICOT Corporation, October 30, 1997, and information from MICOT, January 20, 1997.

[16]W. Stratford, Micro Dot Security Systems, Inc., January 18, 1997.

[17]David A. Eisenberg, Micro Tracers, Inc., presentation to the NRC Committee on Marking, Rendering Inert, and Licensing of Explosive Materials, January 13, 1997, and information from Micro Tracers, Inc.

[18]Science Applications International Corporation, "Detonator Tagging Using Multi-Photon Detection," letter to the NRC Committee on Marking, Rendering Inert, and Licensing of Explosive Materials, 1996.

the emission of multiple high-energy photons. This detection system reportedly offers extreme sensitivity, rapid throughput, ease of use, and low operating costs.

Security Features, Inc.

In written testimony,[19] Security Features, Inc., proposed the use of a Code-B MicroTracing System that uses highly uniform microbeads for identification. These microbeads can be of a certain precise size, a certain color or groups of colors, a specific fluorescence, and have paramagnetic qualities, and/or a combination of any of the above.

Special Technologies Laboratory

Based on a JASON report (JASON, 1994), Special Technologies Laboratory studied cobalt-60 as a radioisotope for (active) preblast detection. Experimental research has been initiated for screening baggage. The company's results indicate that the concept is valid and an effective method of detection but has not yet reached acceptable scan times.

SRI International

SRI International has proposed the use of upconverting phosphors—a class of manufactured, spherical particle materials that absorb radiation (such as from laser excitation) at a specific wavelength and then emit radiation, through luminescence, at a shorter wavelength.[20] The concept has been proposed for both preblast and postblast detection of explosives and has been successfully tested by SRI on a small-scale explosive charge. A larger-scale test is planned.

Tri-Valley Research

Tri-Valley Research proposed using rare-earth (lanthanide) element mixtures to tag explosives for identification.[21] Detection and analysis of these ingredients in explosives would be through x-ray fluorescence spectroscopy.

---

[19]G. Woodward, Security Features, Inc., February 28, 1997.

[20]James Colton, SRI International, presentation to the NRC Committee on Marking, Rendering Inert, and Licensing of Explosive Materials, January 13, 1997, and information from SRI International. See also "Unique Excitation, Emission Forms Basis of New Taggants," *Chemical and Engineering News*, January 27, 1997, p. 24.

[21]John Pearson, Tri-Valley Research, presentation to the NRC Committee on Marking, Rendering Inert, and Licensing of Explosive Materials, January 14, 1997, and information from Tri-Valley Research.

University of Strathclyde, Scotland

In written testimony,[22] the University of Strathclyde, Scotland, proposed selective tagging of explosives using surface enhanced resonance raman scattering as a detection technique.

Urenco Nederland B.V., the Netherlands

In written testimony,[23] Urenco Nederland B.V., the Netherlands, proposed using stable isotopes as a means of tagging explosives.

---

[22]W. Smith and P. White, "Selective Tagging of Explosives Using Surface Enhanced Resonance Raman Scattering (SERRS) as a Detection Technique," University of Strathclyde, Scotland, undated.

[23]Urenco Nederland B.V., information received by the NRC Committee on Marking, Rendering Inert, and Licensing of Explosive Materials, September 25, 1996.

E

Presentations by Stakeholder Groups

The following presentations were made to the Committee on Smokeless and Black Powder during open sessions of meetings on January 14-16, 1998, and March 5-6, 1998.

LAW ENFORCEMENT PRESENTATIONS

Hubert E. Wilson, Bureau of Alcohol, Tobacco, and Firearms (ATF),[1] spoke briefly as a representative of the sponsor of this study. He noted that the ATF was funding the production of this report by congressional mandate, and the ATF did not have an official position on the use of taggants in smokeless or black powders. He also reported that the ATF was in the process of producing its own study on various issues related to the illegal use of explosives, including marking and tagging.

Gregory A. Carl, Federal Bureau of Investigation (FBI),[2] is a hazardous-device examiner and coordinator of postblast investigations. He spoke about the bombing statistics gathered by the FBI, the protocols for evidence gathering, and the jurisdiction of various federal agencies over different types of bombing incidents.

---

[1]Presentation by Hubert E. Wilson, Bureau of Alcohol, Tobacco, and Firearms, January 15, 1998.

[2]Presentation by Gregory A. Carl, Federal Bureau of Investigation, January 15, 1998, and materials distributed to the committee.

The published summary of bombing incidents in 1995 was provided, and the committee heard about how information was gathered through voluntary reporting by local law enforcement personnel. Special Agent Carl noted that smokeless and black powders were used in a significant percentage of the reported improvised explosive devices (roughly one-third), and therefore it was reasonable to consider tagging such powders. He wondered how specific the information from taggants would be, as more specific information is more helpful for obtaining convictions. He said that, without taggants, technicians already are able to identify the brand of powder used in an incident based on unburned powder found at the scene. Currently, the FBI does not have an official position on the use of taggants or on how much information such taggants should contain. Special Agent Carl also expressed concerns about cross-contamination and difficulties in taggant retrieval, as often data collection at bombing scenes is performed by local law enforcement personnel, who do not have access to expensive equipment or extensive training in trace-evidence preservation. The FBI would prefer improved detection technology, as finding and disarming devices before they explode prevents injuries, deaths, and property damage, and preserves evidence. However, bomb squads would always err on the side of caution, so positive or negative signals from markers would not necessarily change the response protocols.

Roger E. Broadbent, Virginia State Police,[3] works with bomb squads and crime scene technicians. The state police support local and federal agencies as needed in both preblast and postblast investigations. He indicated that, as he understood it, taggants could only provide information about the manufacturer of the powder or the date it was produced. Such information would provide limited circumstantial evidence; more useful data could be collected from other parts of the explosive device, such as the pipe, packaging, wires, and so forth. If more detailed information about the powder were to be available, an extensive record-keeping system would be needed, and the last piece of information would depend on the purchaser's willingness to identify himself honestly at the point of sale. Mr. Broadbent expressed concerns about contamination, as a great deal of ammunition is fired legally and would introduce taggants into the environment. He also was worried that if taggants were excluded from certain types of ammunition, such as those used by the police, a black market would develop. Currently, based on his experience with bombing investigations, he believes that most perpetrators purchase commercial powders off the shelf; they do not steal the powders, and they do not make their own.

Anthony Cantu and John Hudson, U.S. Secret Service,[4] spoke about the surveying of buildings for explosive devices in order to ensure the safety of the Presi-

---

[3]Presentation by Roger Broadbent, Virginia State Police, January 15, 1998.
[4]Presentation by Anthony Cantu and John Hudson, U.S. Secret Service, January 15, 1998.

dent of the United States. Canines are currently the most successful tool in detecting explosive materials. The U.S. Secret Service has used technical equipment, but they have not found any machines to be as effective as dogs and human searchers. The main concern of the U.S. Secret Service about taggants or markers would be how these additives would affect the scent of the powders. The variety of explosive materials that canines can be trained on and the degree of sensitivity of these dogs were also discussed.

Lyle O. Malotky, Federal Aviation Administration (FAA),[5] spoke on the detection of explosive materials. He talked about the focus of the FAA on detection of concealed devices within a checkpoint scenario. He described various detection technologies that were split into two types: bulk detection and trace detection. He indicated that the FAA was more concerned with new technologies for the detection of high explosives than for powders, as devices that use powders need containers, which are relatively easy to detect.

Richard A. Strobel, ATF Forensic Science Laboratory,[6] spoke about the variety of roles that the ATF plays in regulating explosive material and investigating incidents involving illegal use of such materials. The ATF runs training sessions for local and state police as well as providing special response teams with bomb scene expertise when requested. ATF trains dogs and keeps statistics on reported bombing incidents. He discussed the protocols for gathering evidence at bomb scenes and the methods used to identify what sort of explosive material was used. In the case of powders, ATF is almost always able to identify the type of propellant and the manufacturing process employed and, in a large number of cases, identify the brand and product line. Such information is used by investigators when they canvass retailers in the area near a bombing to ask about recent sales or to match the type found in a suspect's possession or property. The ATF's current efforts to build a database containing chemical and morphological information on commercially available powders were also described; currently information about roughly 170 powders has been entered.

PRESENTATIONS BY STAKEHOLDERS

John A. Miller, National Muzzleloading Rifle Association (NMRA),[7] spoke on the use of black powder by muzzle loaders nationwide and on their concerns about

---

[5]Presentation by Lyle Malotky, Federal Aviation Administration, January 15, 1998, and materials distributed to the committee.

[6]Presentation by Richard A. Strobel, Bureau of Alcohol, Tobacco, and Firearms, March 5, 1998, and materials distributed to the committee.

[7]Presentation by John A. Miller, National Muzzleloading Rifle Association, January 15, 1998, and materials distributed to the committee.

the addition of foreign substances to the powder. The NMRA members are involved with hunting, shooting competitions, preservation and use of antique firearms, and historical reenactments. They use authentic black powder, as well as black powder substitutes. Mr. Miller discussed concerns about the absence of detailed studies on the safety of introducing taggants into powders, and questions about the effect on the long-term stability of the powders. He also brought up environmental and health issues related to the fact that when a black powder weapon is discharged, a cloud of smoke from the powder is emitted. Finally, he expressed concern that the costs of implementing a record-keeping system to track which taggants are in which cans of powder would be prohibitive and that the actual deterrent effect on criminal activities would be negligible, as potential bombers would obtain the powder by illegal means.

Tanya K. Metaksa, National Rifle Association (NRA),[8] spoke about the legitimate users of smokeless and black powders and the goals and concerns of the NRA related to detecting and identifying explosive materials. She talked about the value of detection technologies and their ability to prevent incidents when deployed widely and effectively. She expressed concerns about the lack of information about taggants' effect on the burning properties of smokeless and black powders (both for reasons of safety and for performance) and mentioned the 1979 explosion of a Goex cast booster plant. She emphasized that the value of taggants as a deterrent was minimal, and the amount of information needed to assist in catching and prosecuting criminals would require a very expensive and complicated record-keeping system. The inclusion of taggants would make the manufacturing, distribution, and use of smokeless and black powders more expensive. She also spoke of the unknown environmental impacts and the potential for countermeasures by those using powders for illegal activities.

James J. Baker and Kenneth D. Green, Sporting Arms and Ammunition Manufacturers' Institute (SAAMI),[9] spoke about the production and use of smokeless powders. Topics discussed included the role of SAAMI in providing standards for ammunition and arms, the size of the domestic market, government regulations about the importation and purchase of powders, stability and performance testing of powders by manufacturers, the amount of powder used in the reloading of ammunition, distribution of powder to commercial customers, and the production of ammunition by large commercial manufacturers.

---

[8]Presentation by Tanya K. Metaksa, National Rifle Association, January 15, 1998, and materials distributed to the committee.

[9]Presentation by James J. Baker and Kenneth D. Green, Sporting Arms and Ammunition Manufacturers' Institute, January 15, 1998, and materials distributed to the committee.

Mick Fahringer, Goex, Inc.,[10] spoke about the manufacture and distribution of black powder. Goex's customers include the pyrotechnics industry, private users (muzzle loading, civil reenactments, competitions), safety fuses (as for model rockets), and the military. Several black powder substitutes are available; these are attractive because they are noncorrosive and burn more cleanly than authentic black powder. He described the various steps for manufacturing black powder. The key characteristics of the finished black powder are the very low moisture content, the specific gravity or hardness, the grain size, and the burn rate. His concerns about introducing taggants into black powder included potential countermeasures, such as removal of the taggants with a magnet or production of homemade black powder, the wide range of granulations of powders that are produced, and the large amount of recycling that occurs in the manufacturing process.

Antonio F. Gonzalez, PRIMEX Technologies,[11] spoke about the manufacture and distribution of smokeless ball powders. PRIMEX produces roughly 120 types of ball powders. He also discussed that PRIMEX occasionally receives requests from the forensic community about identifying a particular sample. PRIMEX is capable of determining which product line it is, but not when it was manufactured. PRIMEX expressed concern regarding the use of taggants for smokeless propellants, particularly with regard to safety of incorporation and handling. The effect of taggants on product performance was also of concern.[12]

James Scheld, Indian Head Division, Naval Surface Warfare Center,[13] spoke about a variety of uses for propellants by the military, specifically about cartridge-actuated devices and propellant-actuated devices. Some examples include ejection seat systems, fire extinguisher systems, and weapons systems. These systems are required to perform with very high reliability and very accurate timing in extreme environments, such as high temperatures and large vibrations. The energetic materials used include pyrotechnic compositions, black powder, single-base and double-base smokeless powders, composite propellants, and high explosives. He also spoke about the military's product specifications for safety, hazard classification, and aging behavior that must be met before any new formulation of propellant may be used in a military device. He described potential

---

[10]Presentation by Mick Fahringer, Goex, Inc., March 5, 1998, and materials distributed to the committee.

[11]Presentation by Antonio F. Gonzalez, PRIMEX Technologies, March 5, 1998, and materials distributed to the committee.

[12]PRIMEX concerns with taggants were expressed during a subcommittee site visit; see Appendix F.

[13]Presentation by James Scheld, Naval Surface Warfare Center, March 5, 1998, and materials distributed to the committee.

impacts of introducing taggants into powders, such as altered performance, altered compatibility with other energetic materials, altered aging characteristics, and increased maintenance and cleaning for multiuse systems, and noted that any changes in powders would require that the military requalify both the powders and the products that use them.

Richard G. Livesay, Consultant,[14] is the inventor of the Microtrace taggant, and he spoke about its history and its use in explosive materials. He described the motivation for its invention and use, and touched on the explosion at the Goex cast booster manufacturing plant in 1979.

ADDITIONAL INPUT

In addition to the presentations listed above, the Committee on Smokeless and Black Powder also received information from those stakeholder groups that made presentations or sent materials to the NRC Committee on Marking, Rendering Inert, and Licensing of Explosive Materials. These stakeholders are listed below, and summaries of their presentations can be found in National Research Council (1998):

- Agricultural Retailers Association,
- American Civil Liberties Union,
- American Iron Ore Association,
- American Portland Cement Alliance,
- American Pyrotechnics Association,
- American Road and Transportation Builders Association,
- Associated Builders and Contractors,
- Austin Powder Company,
- Chemical Manufacturers Association,
- Dyno Nobel, Inc.,
- El Dorado Chemical,
- Glass Packaging Institute,
- Handgun Control, Inc.,
- ICI Explosives,
- Indiana Limestone Institute,
- Institute of Makers of Explosives,
- Intel Corporation,
- International Association of Bomb Technicians and Investigators,
- International Fertilizer Development Center,
- International Society of Explosives Engineers,

---

[14]Presentation by Richard G. Livesay, March 6, 1998.

- Johnson Matthey Electronics,
- La Roche Industries,
- Los Angeles County Sheriff's Department,
- National Industrial Sand Association,
- National Lime Association,
- National Mining Association,
- National Stone Association,
- National Utility Contractors Association,
- The Associated General Contractors of America,
- The Fertilizer Institute,
- The Gypsum Association, and
- Wiley, Rein & Fielding (representing UNIMIN, a supplier of high-quality silica used in semiconductor manufacturing).

F

Committee Site Visits

ALLIANT TECHSYSTEMS/NEW RIVER ENERGETICS

Edwin P. Przybylowicz, Karl V. Jacob, Walter F. Rowe, Ronald L. Simmons, and Judith B. Snow, Committee Members

A subcommittee of the Committee on Smokeless and Black Powder[1] met with Paul Furrier (commercial market manager), E. Hays Zeigler (staff engineer), and Rob Allen (manager, business and operations support, Smokeless Powder Group) on March 4, 1998, in Radford, Virginia.

Facility

The Radford facility was built as a U.S. Army facility in 1941. Alliant (Hercules prior to 1995) signed a facility use agreement with the Army, and in August of 1996 began moving their operations to Radford from their plant in Kenvil, New Jersey. At the time of the visit, the solvent recovery facility was not yet operational, but production was taking place. New River Energetics is a wholly owned subsidiary of Alliant Techsystems. The Radford site is a government-owned, contractor-operated facility.

The subcommittee observed the manufacturing process from the dehydration

---

[1]National Research Council staff members Elizabeth L. Grossman and Christopher K. Murphy also attended this site visit.

of nitrocellulose (NC) to the final packaging of the finished powder, but did not have the opportunity to observe the ballistics testing. Each step of the manufacturing process is isolated in its own individual building in order to minimize damage and injury in the event of an accident.

Smokeless Powder Overview

The major ingredients of smokeless powder include NC and nitroglycerin (NG). Minor ingredients consist of stabilizers, plasticizers, flash suppressants, deterrents, and dyes and opacifiers. Other minor ingredients include graphite glaze, bore erosion reduction coatings, and ignition aid coatings. Together, the minor ingredients make up roughly 2 or 3 percent of the finished powder. The major monitored characteristics of gun propellants are burn-rate characteristics, geometry, and propellant design for specific applications. New River has a few hundred smokeless powder formulations, of which roughly 60 to 70 are in active use. There are 13 different Alliant reloading powder types.

New River Energetics Powder Process

The process employed by Alliant Techsystems for the production of smokeless powder begins with the dehydration of 28 percent water-wet NC by replacement of the water with ethyl alcohol. The dehydrated NC in the form of blocks is broken up, and a portion is mixed with NG to form a pre-mix. A weighed amount of pre-mix, together with "broken" NC is added to a mixer and is mixed with solvents and other ingredients to form the specific powder. This is followed by extrusion/cutting and then coating/glazing. The powder is then dried, screened, and homogenized. Subsequent to the mixing step, contamination between different formulations of smokeless powder is possible. The powder is packed into sublots and placed in a rest house. The ballistics are tested, and a final blend sequence occurs before packing and shipping the powders. In the final blending, a nonconforming part of the lot could be pulled out and reworked later. Production of a 10,000-pound lot is performed in approximately 1,000-pound increments. Products in the rest house could go to 10 to 15 different products. There is a potential for and likely small, inevitable amounts of contamination during each of these stages.

To aid in identifying certain powders to reloaders, Alliant manufactures grades of smokeless powders that contain dyed powder particles. These include Red-, Blue-, and Green-Dot smokeless powders. The dyed particles make up about 1 percent of the total mixture and are ballistically identical to the powders to which they are added. The dyed blends are produced separately and are mixed into the undyed products at the final blend.

Commercial Smokeless Powder Market

The domestic market for smokeless powder includes original equipment manufacturer (OEM) customers, individual reloaders, and specialty device manufacturers, such as makers of airbags. The smaller export market consists of OEM customers and individual reloaders. Two domestic manufacturers and six foreign manufacturers import smokeless powder into the United States. Distribution occurs through the two domestic manufacturers and six other companies. OEM customers include major ammunition manufacturers, smaller ammunition manufacturers, and custom reloading operations.

Distribution of smokeless powder from Alliant goes to six regional master powder distributors. From there, the powder is sent to smaller distributors and wholesalers, who then sell smokeless powder to retail dealers, gun shops, gun clubs, and hardware stores, as well as to individual reloaders.

The smokeless powder shipped by Alliant stays intact through the final sale, with no mixing. Though not recommended, end users may mix on their own after purchasing the powder. When shipping from Alliant, lots are broken and are sent to more than one master distributor. Each individual container of smokeless powder has a lot number and date of packing. These records are kept for approximately 3 years. A sample of each lot is kept for about 5 years for quality assurance purposes.

PRIMEX TECHNOLOGIES, INC.

*Leo R. Gizzi, Janice M. Hiroms, Ronald L. Simmons, and
Raymond S. Voorhees, Committee Members*

A subcommittee of the Committee on Smokeless and Black Powder[2] visited the production facilities of PRIMEX Technologies, Inc., on March 17, 1998. Tony Gonzalez, director of Research and Development, hosted the visit.

History of PRIMEX Operations

The PRIMEX facility in St. Marks, Florida, manufactures single-base and double-base smokeless propellants for commercial and military applications using the BALL POWDER® propellant process. This is a patented process (developed in the 1930s by Western Cartridge Corporation in East Alton, Illinois), and is unlike any other process for making smokeless powder. Olin was the owner of Western Cartridge, which later became a part of its Winchester Division. The propellant business is now a part of PRIMEX Technologies. Olin has licensed the

---

[2]Staff member Gregory Eyring also attended this site visit.

process to at least 10 other companies and governments worldwide to manufacture powder for commercial and military purposes.

The St. Marks plant started operations in 1970. Its total capacity is 12 million to 16 million pounds per year, depending on the product mix. It is estimated that current production is less than 10 million pounds per year, with about 2 million pounds going to the military. The amount diverted to military ammunition varies considerably.

PRIMEX sells BALL POWDER® propellant commercially to ammunition manufacturers, master distributors, and repackagers who, in turn, sell it in 1- to 8-pound canisters through master distributors to about 6,000 retail outlets. Thus, PRIMEX estimated that one production lot could conceivably be distributed to in excess of 15,000 customers. PRIMEX estimates there are about 3 million consumers of canister powder in the United States.

The BALL POWDER® Process

The BALL POWDER® propellant process is unique and quite different from the conventional process for making smokeless powder. NC—either freshly made or recovered—plus a stabilizer is dissolved in hot ethyl acetate to form a viscous doughlike lacquer that is then extruded through a perforated plate with die-face cutting blades into water, forming spherical globules of various sizes.

Additional process steps include better defining the spherical grain through solvent removal, impregnation with NG, deterrent coating, and calendar rolling to flatten the spheres to a desired thickness. Rework levels of up to 40 percent, depending on product mix, are reincorporated into the production process at the first step (NC lacquer formation). Rework may even include final products that may be remnants or unusable material. Production is a batch process at this stage.

Eventually, the BALL POWDER® propellant is dried, glazed with graphite, blended, and packaged for shipment. After the initial drying stage, the powders undergo extensive gun ballistic testing and blending to achieve the desired ballistic performance. (The primary specification required by the user is gun ballistics, not chemical composition. Blending and recycling of blends is extensive to attain the proper ballistics.)

From a historical perspective, the original patented BALL POWDER® propellant process was a batch process that produced a spherical precipitated globule of limited size and hence useful only to a limited range of gun calibers. Eventually, process and product technology enhancements expanded the applicability and use of BALL POWDER® propellants to a wide variety of applications.

In general, PRIMEX makes BALL POWDER® propellants in two different densities: a high-density product and a low-density product. Porosity is deliberately introduced to increase the "burning speed" of low-density propellants. Both density products are made in general size ranges, yielding a variety of different density-size base grains. Different amounts of NG are introduced (ranging from 0 to 40 percent) and different concentrations of deterrent coating applied (ranging from 0 to 10 percent), totaling over 120 different BALL POWDER® propellants for a wide variety of applications.

The final quality criterion in the production of smokeless powder is performance in ballistics tests, which can be achieved by blending and reblending of stocks that may differ in composition by a few percent in various ingredients. Chemical composition is controlled at different levels for different components.

The PRIMEX operation features extensive recycling and reuse of both process solvent and process water back into the manufacturing steps, such that there is virtually nothing discharged into the air or surrounding water streams. The process requires tremendous amount of process water.

A "Lab Practical"

PRIMEX has cooperated in the past with the ATF and the FBI in assisting them with the identification of ball powders. One committee member brought small samples of spherical gunpowder from two bombing cases under active investigation, to test the extent to which a manufacturer such as PRIMEX can identify powders from inherent morphological and chemical characteristics.

One sample was collected from the scene of an actual explosion, while the other two samples were collected from different, unexploded, improvised explosive devices that had been rendered safe. The questions to PRIMEX involved product identification and the degree of certainty to which two unburned samples could be distinguished as being of the same type.

The burned sample from the exploded device was examined microscopically by three chemists in the Research and Development Analytical Laboratory at PRIMEX. Each declared that it did not appear to be a PRIMEX product. High-performance liquid chromatography analyses (two independent examinations) produced results that strongly suggested it was not PRIMEX-made gunpowder. One of their chemists stated that the powder "looked to be Chinese." This information would imply a likely powder source if it were purchased domestically.

The two unburned samples were examined by liquid chromatography and Fourier transform infrared analyses. No meaningful differences could be observed between the two, leading to the conclusion that the two "could be of common origin"—under the circumstances, probably the strongest conclusion that would stand up in court. According to the PRIMEX chemists, the powder "looked and analyzed" like their WSX® 110 canistered product, leading them to the conclusion that it was in fact a PRIMEX product. It should be noted that similar powder may also be found in loaded ammunition. This "lab practical" demonstrated that currently available techniques can often identify the product type for domestic commercial powders.

NATIONAL RIFLE ASSOCIATION HEADQUARTERS

Edwin P. Przybylowicz, Leo R. Gizzi,Walter F. Rowe, and
Ronald L. Simmons, Committee Members

On March 18, 1998, a subcommittee of the Committee on Smokeless and Black Powder[3] visited the National Rifle Association (NRA) Headquarters in Fairfax, Virginia, to learn about the reloading process using smokeless powder and to observe the use of black powder in muzzle-loading rifles. Tammy Begun, Michael Bussard, William Parkerson, and Glenn Gilbert hosted this visit.

Reloading Process

The reloading procedure of 12 gauge shotgun shells, 9 mm pistol bullets and .30 caliber (7.62 mm) rifle bullets was demonstrated to the subcommittee. Reloading was indicated as a procedure used by a number of target shooters to reduce the cost of their ammunition (typically by 50 percent), to provide experimental loads for better performance, to match a load to a specific gun, and for recreational enjoyment.

The manual equipment used to reload this ammunition consisted basically of a series of dies contained on a platen or a "press" that permitted the following steps to be performed on the initially empty, used shell casing: (1) remove the spent primer and resize the casing to remove deformations from previous use; (2) install a new primer; (3) add a measured amount of smokeless powder; (4) seat and crimp the bullet, or in the case of a shotgun shell to add the plastic "wad" (which separates the powder from the shot); (5) add a measured amount of shot; (6) in the case of a shotgun shell, pre-crimp the top of the plastic shell casing; and (7) finish the crimping of the top of the shell. The first three steps are basically the same for shotgun shells and ammunition for pistols and rifles. In the case of the shotgun shells, a shell casing is used—a plastic tube with a brass base—into which the primer is mounted. In the latter two cases, the shell casing is brass, and because bullets instead of shot are used, there is no need for a wad separator. In these cases, the bullet is added after addition of powder.

It was observed that reloading shells must be done according to a tested formula that is carefully spelled out in reloading manuals, so that the correct propellant is used in the specified amounts. The equipment for reloading is typically sold through retail gun shops, rather than mass merchant chains. The manual equipment generally sells for under $100, although there are semiautomated devices that cost more. Safety instruction in the use of this equipment is

---

[3]NRC staff members Douglas J. Raber, Elizabeth L. Grossman, Gregory Eyring, Christopher K. Murphy, and David Grannis also attended this site visit.

provided at the point of sale by the retailer. The manual that comes with the equipment has a section on safely using this equipment. In comparing it with instruction manuals that come with shop equipment, the emphasis on safety is no greater than that one might find with a table saw, perhaps even less. For reloaders who seek more information, more detailed instruction manuals and videos may be purchased separately.

One of the powders demonstrated was Alliant Red Dot, which has a small percentage of red colored particles in it to identify the product. When asked whether this was not a type of taggant, the response was that those particles were in fact active powder with a small amount of dye on the surface.

There was also a discussion of rimfire ammunition such as .22 caliber long-rifle ammunition. Rimfire ammunition does not have a separate primer component like centerfire ammunition, but instead has primer material in the rim of the cartridge case base. The firing pin strikes the base of the cartridge at the rim, crushing the primer mix between the cartridge case wall and rim, thus igniting it, and in succession, the smokeless powder. Because the rim of the cartridge case is permanently deformed by firing, it is not reusable. Some primer compositions have a small amount of very fine ground glass added to increase the sensitivity and improve reliability of ignition. The presence of ground glass reportedly increases barrel erosion and reduces barrel life. Because of its simplicity, rimfire ammunition is considerably lower in cost than centerfire ammunition, and is used solely for .22 caliber.

Shooting demonstrations were carried out with a muzzle-loading rifle, a semiautomatic centerfire rifle (M-1A), and a Glock semiautomatic centerfire pistol.

The NRA reported that they do carry out some instrumental measurements in the firing range, measuring for velocity and accuracy. Ammunition manufacturers normally carry out such measurements and chamber pressure measurements to ensure that they are meeting the specifications of the Sporting Arms and Ammunition Manufacturers' Institute (SAAMI).

Advantages of Reloading

Following the subcommittee site visit to the National Rifle Association headquarters, the committee received information from SAAMI and the National Reloading Manufacturers' Association regarding reloading.[4] The following points were made regarding the advantages of reloading of smokeless and black powders over purchasing factory-loaded ammunition.

---

[4]Written materials received from Robert Delfay, Sporting Arms and Ammunition Manufacturers' Institute, and Bill Chevalier, National Reloading Manufacturers' Association, on June 12, 1998.

• *Cost.* It is roughly half the cost to reload a cartridge compared to purchasing a factory round. The brass case (for centerfire ammunition) and the shotshell hull (for shotgun shooting) are the most expensive components of ammunition, and both can be reused several times when reloading. The other components of ammunition can only be used once, but are less costly than the casings. As sport shooters, target shooters, and hunters often shoot many thousands of rounds per year, the savings due to reloading can be substantial compared with purchasing ammunition for roughly $0.75 per round.

• *Performance.* Depending on the intended use of the ammunition, powder type and quantity can be adjusted to give higher or lower pressures and bullet velocities. Reloading can enhance shooting accuracy and performance, as well as reduce gun fouling.

• *Precision.* Many shooters reload to gain precision between rounds. Depending on the type of shooting, the ability to reproduce velocities and trajectories can be crucial to the reloader.

• *Components.* Some reloaders prefer the ability to choose the specific powder, casings, primers, and bullets in each round of ammunition. This choice of components may be based on increased performance or special needs of a shooter.

BUREAU OF ALCOHOL, TOBACCO, AND FIREARMS NATIONAL LABORATORY CENTER

*Edwin P. Przybylowicz, Margaret A. Berger, Leo R.Gizzi,
Walter F. Rowe, and Ronald L. Simmons, Committee Members*

On March 19, 1998, a subcommittee of the Committee on Smokeless and Black Powder[5] visited the National Laboratory Center of the Bureau of Alcohol, Tobacco and Firearms (ATF) in Rockville, Maryland, to learn more about the forensic process used in bombing incidents. Richard A. Strobel, forensic chemist, Explosives Section, and Cynthia L. Wallace, forensic chemist, hosted this visit.

The subcommittee heard an overview of the ATF forensic group's process in handling typical cases, including how the combination of physical, chemical, and other evidence is brought together in resolving the case.

There was discussion of cases in which going back to the retail outlet where a powder was purchased had provided leads in states where the law requires the signature of the purchaser, although very few states are reported to have this requirement.

The subcommittee also observed some of the reference information that the ATF was in the process of developing. This consists of examining commercial

---

[5]NRC staff members Christopher K. Murphy and David Grannis also attended this site visit.

powders from various manufacturers for physical characteristics such as shape and size of particles and looking at the variability among lots of the same product. In addition to physical characterization, the powders are put through high-performance liquid chromatography to provide a qualitative picture of the major and minor components in the powder. Analysis of these data has demonstrated that while size characterization can be used to narrow down the identification of commercial powders, it is not always possible to use qualitative chromatography for such characterizations. Decomposition of the powders during a variety of storage conditions gives significant variation in the chromatograms, and it has been concluded that more quantitative analysis must be used in the chromatography.

Commercial powders do not retain the same chemical and sometimes physical characteristics from batch to batch; blending, multiple sourcing of components, and using both domestic and foreign finished powders make mixtures that may perform according to product specifications but that can vary considerably in composition.

Despite the complexities in the characterization of powders to determine their origin, the ATF reports that in a very high percentage of the cases, it is successful in identifying the type and manufacturing source of powder used in a bomb. It sometimes may take considerable effort to accomplish this, but nonetheless the success rate is high.

It was pointed out that the development of a computerized reference library of information is still in its early stages and is being coordinated with the FBI Chemistry Unit Laboratory. There is no comprehensive program to obtain samples from all propellant manufacturers for use in a database, despite the fact that American producers seem willing to provide such samples. ATF agents periodically visit some U.S. powder manufacturers in the course of normal casework, but the effort falls short of a systematic accumulation of existing data on commercially manufactured powders. Similarly, there is little public statistical information on the production of the various powders, as a means of more easily interpreting results obtained in the forensic examination and relating it to the availability of certain powders. ATF agents acknowledged that information on powder characteristics, variations, and distribution of currently used commercial powders in a statistical database would provide an invaluable reference source for interpreting forensic results.

In response to questions, the forensic chemists volunteered the information that the current commercial identification of some powders with dyed propellant particles (Red Dot, Blue Dot, and Green Dot) provides useful leads in identifying the commercial source of the powder used.

The ATF also described how all details beyond the chemistry of the propellant are used in a bombing case to establish leads. This was illustrated with a microswitch from the detonation mechanism that ATF forensic chemists were piecing together in order to reconstruct a part number. Such information is often used to solicit further information from commercial outlets, such as electronic part retailers, who may record the customers' names and addresses. In a number of cases, such forensic information is reported to have been useful in identifying a store. This can be helpful if a bomber has purchased electronic parts that were used in making a device.

The subcommittee was shown how the physical characterization of pipe fragmentation can be used to narrow down the possible propellants used in the pipe bomb. The portable chromatographic system, Aegis—a device that can be fitted to a laboratory trailer for transportation to a bombing scene to enable efficient processing of information at a bombing site—was observed.

The forensic identification of the commercial powder used in a pipe bomb is of great importance as it may help in directing field agents to locating and apprehending the perpetrator. The identification of the powder may currently take time and effort due to the varied nature and source of the powders. An investigation would be significantly aided by a fast identification of the commercial propellant used in the bomb.

It was pointed out that identifying the commercial source of a powder is but one step in the investigation process leading to the indictment of a perpetrator. Such information is used to direct field agents in the search for additional evidence leading to a suspect. Until and unless a linkage can be made between the propellant found at a bombing site and that in possession of the suspect, this evidence cannot contribute to the suspect's conviction. The importance of this evidentiary link would also be strengthened by a statistical analysis of the likelihood of a suspect's possessing a specific type of powder. Currently, there is in some cases insufficient evidence to obtain a search warrant of the suspect's premises.

FEDERAL BUREAU OF INVESTIGATION, EXPLOSIVES AND CHEMISTRY UNITS

Edwin P. Przybylowicz, Margaret A. Berger, Leo R. Gizzi,
Walter F. Rowe, and Ronald L. Simmons, Committee Members

On March 19, 1998, a subcommittee of the Committee on Smokeless and Black Powder[6] visited the Explosives and Chemistry Units of the Federal Bureau of Investigation (FBI) in Washington, D.C., to learn more about the forensic process used in bombing incidents. Greg A. Carl (Special Agent), Kelly Mount, and Ron Kelley hosted the visit.

The subcommittee toured parts of the laboratory, starting with the office where all evidence is received. This office receives sealed packages from the mailroom in the FBI building and establishes an audit trail that the evidence will

---

[6]NRC staff members Christopher K. Murphy and David Grannis also attended this site visit.

follow while in the laboratory. This unit receives samples not only from FBI agents across the country, but also from local and state law enforcement units, for whom the FBI carries out free analyses. Received packages are first examined to establish their integrity; if it appears that the evidence may have been compromised in any way, through cross-contamination or poor packaging, for example, it is returned to the sender with the indication that no work will be done on the material. At the receiving office, the evidence is assigned to the one agent who is likely to have most of the work on a given case. This person is responsible for coordinating all of the work carried out on the evidence. The procedures established within the FBI to maintain the integrity of the evidence while it is analyzed were shown in detail. Care is taken to avoid contamination of the evidence, and one case at a time is worked on in a given laboratory area.

The subcommittee toured the various laboratories and was shown a chemistry laboratory equipped with modern analytical instrumentation.[7] There was discussion of the reference material on propellants that the FBI is working on with the ATF National Laboratory Center. The FBI displayed a sample entry from its powder database, containing statistical information, a typical analytical spectra, and a photograph of the powder. As with the ATF, FBI investigations of explosive devices containing smokeless or black powder seek to identify the propellant and its source. While the FBI receives cooperation from the propellant manufacturers, full collaboration has not been realized; the effort made on reference materials and collaboration is secondary to casework (see also site visit to ATF).

Despite the complexities in the characterization of powder to determine their origin, the FBI laboratory reports that they are successful in identifying the type and manufacturing source of powder used in a very high percentage of bombing cases. It sometimes may take them considerable effort to accomplish this, but nonetheless their success rate is high.

When asked about differences in the FBI compared to the ATF laboratories in specific bombing investigations, the answer centered around response time and detailed analyses. The FBI personnel report that their laboratory "has more forensic resources at its disposal which would allow a more thorough analysis of the evidence."[8]

Smokeless Powder Database

The FBI and the ATF have compiled a database with information on smokeless and black powders. This computerized database consists of a list of ingredients in a variety of commercially available smokeless and black powders. In

---

[7]Separate laboratories exist for different fields of forensic science; there are offices for work on writing analysis, explosives, product tampering, and so forth.

[8]Personal communication following site visit from Special Agent Gregory Carl, July 29, 1998.

addition, the two agencies have a noncomputerized listing for a number of powders. This contains photographs of powder morphology, and a gas chromatography trace for the powders.

On the issue of taggants, Ron Kelley stated that taggants would aid in distinguishing between powder A and powder B. He did not believe that having a date of manufacture for a powder used in a bomb would help much in an investigation. He said that at present, having the red dot (blue dot and so forth) in the powder helps tremendously in identifying the manufacturer. He added that in about 97 percent of the cases, ready identification is possible of the type and brand of the powder used in bombings, but that the other 3 percent present difficulties. He also said that over 90 percent of the bombing cases examined by the FBI involve smokeless and black powders.

GOEX, INC.

Leo R. Gizzi, Karl V. Jacob, Roger L. Schneider, Judith B. Snow, and Ronald R. Vandebeek, Committee Members

A subcommittee of the Committee on Smokeless and Black Powder[9] visited Goex, Inc., the only black powder manufacturer in North America, on April 22, 1998. The subcommittee met with Goex president Mick Fahinger, and Don MacDonald, vice president of operations. It received a description of the manufacturing and distribution process but did not directly observe the facility.

Black Powder Manufacturing

The first step in the manufacturing process involves intimate mixing of charcoal, sulfur, and potassium (or sodium) nitrate. This is accomplished at Goex, Inc., through the use of wheel mills. The Chinese are known to use ball mills, which are acceptable but less capable of achieving such mixing. The ingredients are used straight from the manufacturer, with no preprocessing. The sulfur and charcoal come in supersacks and are introduced into a ball mill. The resulting pulverized material is then emptied from the drum through a screen, and a conveyer carries it over to a magnet to remove any ferromagnetic material. It is then put into sacks. The pulverized material is then mixed with potassium nitrate and a fixed amount of water. The ingredients are mixed into a wheel cake by crushing, using an 11,000-pound wheel mill. The water content is essential because with too much water, the wheels slip, and with too little water, the powder becomes too fine. The mixture is contained in a pan during this process.

---

[9]NRC staff member Christopher K. Murphy also attended this site visit.

The compression point is between the base of the wheel and the top surface of the pan. This entire process is performed remotely for a specific period of time.

The wheel cake is then taken to the press. The friable wheel cake, including 2 percent water, passes through a chute over another magnet into the box, past breakdown rolls. Next, 113 aluminum plates are placed in the box of the press, each 2 feet square, held in position by a set of slotted finger boards. Once the box is filled, the finger boards are removed. What remains is a box filled with wheel cake separated into compartments, 3/4 inch thick, by the aluminum plate partitions. The hydraulic ram then compresses the wheel cake three times. This is a dusty operation. For the first ram, a certain number of plates and wheel cake are present in the box; additional wheel cake and plates are then added for the second "push"; and finally the remaining plates and cake are added for the third push. At the end of the operation, the box contains the 113 aluminum plates and the compressed cakes of black powder, 3/4 inch thick and 2 feet square.

The next step in the process is the corning mill, where granulation takes place. A first screening is done, where distribution of the granulations depends on the size of the screens used in the shaker. The black powder is then taken up in a lift and dumped into a hopper. An aluminum shaker with screens oscillates at 123 rpm. Powder that does not pass through the screens is returned to the rolls through a bucket elevator. All of the chutes contain magnets. The corning mill has many more moving parts than any other equipment in the plant. The process contains many trips to stop the process.

For the approximately 40 percent of black powder that is glazed, the usual coating is graphite. The powder is rotated in wooden barrels for 8 hours at a temperature of 180 ºC. Graphite is added in quantities of about 5 pounds for 3,000-pound batches of black powder. Drying during this process produces a black powder with less than 1 percent water content. Black powder produced for pyrotechnics is unglazed.

The final step is sifting, where the powder is passed through wooden cabinets on a shaft containing 15 screens. Following this step, the powder is packaged. The powder is placed in buggies and put into packaging hoppers. These hoppers produce 1-pound packages. A serious problem in the process comes from lightning, and Goex has an advanced Doppler radar warning system installed. The entire manufacturing process from wheeling to packaging takes about 3 days.

Each batch of black powder produced is burn tested by placing a fixed amount of powder in a fixed length of lead tube. The tube is timed to see how long it takes to burn. There is a great deal of consistency between various batches of the same type of black powder produced at Goex. Specific gravity of the powder is also measured.

The subcommittee was shown different grain sizes of black powder for use in a diverse set of applications. For example, the coarse grains are used in military ammunition; fine grains are used by muzzle-loading shooters; and both fine and coarse grains are used in pyrotechnics for both lift and burst charges. There are 60 different types of grains manufactured by Goex.

WINCHESTER AMMUNITION PLANT

Edwin P. Przybylowicz, Leo R. Gizzi, Per-Anders Persson, and Ronald L. Simmons, Committee Members

On May 22, 1998, a subcommittee of the Committee on Smokeless and Black Powder[10] visited the Winchester Ammunition Plant in East Alton, Illinois. The subcommittee met with Tim Vaitekunas, manager of ballistic services; T. Valdez, manager of rimfire; C. Phillips, manager of centerfire; R. Green, manager of shotshell; G. Boeker, manager of distribution; and J. Rodden, director of quality.

The visit reviewed the manufacturing and distribution operations that relate to the flow of propellant into the manufacture of ammunition and subsequent packaging and distribution. Winchester uses both domestic and imported (from domestic distributors) smokeless powder in their ammunition. Winchester does, however, make its own priming mixture, which is a pyrotechnic. Powders are purchased on the basis of both quality and economy and are used for one or more applications. Certification of the powders is done by the seller, though Winchester does audit the powder they purchase. For smokeless powder sold to reloaders, every lot is tested at Winchester.

Winchester has specified that propellant supplied for their production should not contain added salt (to control muzzle flash) nor other additives that can segregate in transport and under conditions where the powder is shaken. Even without additives, some powders segregate in shipping, which results in fines that must be removed or the lot will be rejected. It was mentioned that some manufacturers are supplying this very fine propellant as "primer additive." Segregation also occurs in certain operations during the loading of some propellant lots.

The subcommittee viewed ammunition manufacturing operations in rimfire, centerfire, and shotshell operations starting with the receiving of the powder from the powder magazine to the finished shell. The operations were automated with the higher volume (rimfire and centerfire) shells being very highly productive, automated machines. For shotgun shells, the increased number of components, and larger size of the shell leads to a comparatively lower production of shells per unit time. In all cases the steps in the operation were similar: positioning of the shell (with primer coating or centerfire primer preloaded), loading of powder, insertion of bullet (or wad, if a shotgun shell), crimping the bullet in the casing (or adding the shot to a shotgun shell and crimping the plastic casing at the top).

---

[10]NRC staff member Christopher K. Murphy also attended this site visit.

Once the bullets were loaded they were then packaged in the appropriate containers (either plastic holders, cardboard boxes, or tool cartridges for the industrial market).

Hundreds of millions of centerfire ammunitions rounds are produced per year. For rimfire ammunition, the number is even greater, on the order of billions of rounds per year.

Testing and inspection took place at several places along the manufacturing line. Testing is done to ensure that the ammunition meets specifications. Incoming propellant must meet certification standards before it is loaded by Winchester, so it undergoes ballistic tests and is approved for loading. Ammunition manufacture is a batch or continuous operation. The high-volume products are continuous operation. Different batches of the same powder may be used in the continuous run, thus more than one batch may be used in some ammunition manufacture in a given day. The code marked on the box of packaged ammunition is a date of loading code, which would allow tracing to find what batches of powder were used in that day's production. However, in the present system, it would not be possible to relate which batch of powder was used in a given box of ammunition, if several powder batches were used on a given day in the manufacture of a particular type of ammunition. The manufacturing operations run on three shifts with either 5- or 6-day operations, depending on the time of year, since some segments of the market are seasonal.

Testing identifies ammunition that does not meet standards for any one of a number of reasons. Ballistic tests may raise questions about certain samples of ammunition. For shotgun shells, ballistics testing checked both pressure and velocity. Additional testing was done to check for any imperfections in the performance of the shell in the shotgun. Any material not meeting specifications is set aside for future rework. The reworking results in such ammunition either being brought into specifications and then entering the packaging and distribution system at a later date (with a later, or no loading date code). In a small percentage of cases, the suspect ammunition cannot be salvaged and is scrapped.

The continuous manufacturing operation plus the rework pattern results in some small percentage of ammunition being shipped without the loading date code that allows tracing to a lot, or group of lots, of propellant that is loaded into that particular ammunition on a particular date.

The distribution center receives boxed ammunition from production with the date of loading on the box. The distribution center puts its own identifying code on the box, which identifies the product type and manufacturer but does not carry any of the manufacturing information related to the lot of the propellant, and so forth, on it. After distribution, if ammunition is determined to have a functional problem, the only recourse the manufacturer has is to publicize to the distributors and retailers the box code, which is the date of loading, and request a recall. The company has no records as to where specific boxes of ammunition have been distributed. In later discussions, questions were raised regarding what would be entailed in setting up such a system. Not only would the record keeping in the distribution system become more complex, but the cost of cleaning equipment between lot changes of propellant would present major problems in a manufacturing system not designed to be easily purged of previously used propellant. The added cost of doing this was deemed to be prohibitively high (speculation was that the increase would range from a factor of 2 to an order of magnitude). Winchester does, however, presently maintain records of lot numbers, for example, for as long as 20 to 25 years.

When asked about Winchester's participation in forensic investigations, the staff indicated that they get about 30 inquiries in a year, which most often are attempts to identify whether a fragment of spent ammunition is from a Winchester product. Questions regarding the propellant are most often referred to propellant manufacturers.

HODGDON POWDER COMPANY

Margaret A. Berger, Leo R. Gizzi, Karl V. Jacob, Roger L. Schneider, and Ronald L. Simmons, Committee Members

On May 29, 1998, a subcommittee of the Committee on Smokeless and Black Powder[11] visited the Hodgdon Powder Company in Shawnee Mission, Kansas. Ben Barrett (manager, engineering & safety), Doug Delsemme (vice president and general counsel), George Webber (manager of ballistics), and Bob Blattman (magazine manager) hosted the visit.

Hodgdon Powder Company is a wholesale distributor of smokeless powder that does not sell powder directly to the public. Hodgdon currently sells 25 different powders under its own label—16 rifle powders and 9 powders for shotgun and pistol. They are also master distributors for Alliant and Winchester. Hodgdon does not manufacture smokeless powder, although it does repackage smokeless powder from PRIMEX (at St. Marks, Florida), surplus government military powder, and powder imported from Australia. A lot number and date of packaging is stamped on each packaged canister, caddie, and keg (all are conductive plastic bottles or jugs). The lot number and date go both on the individual package and the larger box that the canisters are shipped in. A record is made of the quantity packed on each date for a particular lot. These records are maintained indefinitely. When filling an order, the amount and lot number are noted on a data sheet.

The powder is stored and packaged in 25 buildings located on 70 acres. The packaging is in 1-pound canisters, 5-pound caddies, and 8-pound kegs. These operations have been in Shawnee since 1954. The company was founded by

---

[11]NRC staff member Christopher K. Murphy also attended this site visit.

Bruce Hodgdon in 1946 to repackage surplus military smokeless powder for the shooting market.

Smokeless powder is dispensed manually (and remotely from behind a barricade) from a hopper containing about 30 to 50 pounds of powder. The hopper is lined with conductive Velostat® plastic, which is cleaned with high-pressure air before a different powder is used. Excess powder, which typically is less than a 1-pound canister for each lot, is collected, and given to a local fire department, which burns it for demonstrations. Excess powder thus is destroyed rather than recycled. Admixing of powder from different incoming lots does occur, and Hodgdon continues to purchase government military surplus powders, which is how they started in 1952. Each incoming lot is accepted on certification from the manufacturer per Hodgdon specifications, and is randomly tested for ballistics before repackaging. All repacked lots are tested for ballistics in several different cartridges before shipment. The plant operates one shift, 5 days per week. The ballistics laboratory also conducts research and development on new cartridges, as well as seeking better powders to use in existing cartridges of ammunition.

There are numerous magazines where packaged/boxed containers of smokeless powder are stored prior to shipment. Also stored in magazines is smokeless powder received from the propellant manufacturers for repackaging: Alliant, PRIMEX, ADI Limited (Australia), and military surplus powder. Each of the containers from the propellant manufacturer has a lot number, packed date, and powder designation (name).

Hodgdon ships its repackaged smokeless powders to several hundred different distributors nationwide, which in turn ship to retailers. A typical lot goes to many distributors, depending on the market. In addition to the domestic distributors, Hodgdon exports smokeless powder to 12 foreign countries. Smokeless powder is shipped as DOT 1.3 C Powder, Explosive, or as DOT 4.1 Flammable Solid, depending on the packaging.

The subcommittee toured the ballistics laboratory, where testing is done in Sporting Arms and Ammunition Manufacturers' Institute pressure barrels, using piezoelectric gages and/or the older copper crusher method. Each different cartridge is fired from a different barrel. Lot acceptance testing involves 10 cartridges from each lot, and the results are compared to 10 reference shots. In addition to room-temperature conditioning (for a minimum of 24 hours) for gun ballistics, testing at extreme temperatures of -20 °F and +125 °F is done periodically.

Hodgdon also manufactures and markets a black powder substitute known as Pyrodex, which is claimed to have 30 percent more power than black powder. Pyrodex is loaded by equivalent volume to black powder by using a handheld volumetric measure. Pyrodex is manufactured in Herington, Kansas, about 100 miles southwest of Kansas City, and is offered in four grades, including consolidated pellets for ease of loading. Pyrodex is a patented product introduced to the shooting market in 1976. Discussions of the Pyrodex manufacturing process are proprietary.

G

Laboratories Capable of Testing

The Committee on Smokeless and Black Powder was asked to identify at least three organizations capable of testing how markers or taggants affect the performance of black and smokeless powders (see Appendix B).

TYPES OF TESTING NEEDED

The tests necessary to quantify the performance of these powders fall into two broad categories: quality tests and ballistics tests. The first set of tests focuses on the chemical and physical behavior of the powder before it is loaded into ammunition or fireworks. Chemical tests include accelerated aging tests, stabilizer depletion tests, chemical reactivity tests, differential scanning calorimetry, and variable-temperature compatibility and stability tests. The physical tests include impact, friction, electrostatic discharge, impingement, critical height (to explosion), segregation, and flow/bulk density.[1] Ballistics tests focus on the performance of the powders in standard usages, such as ammunition or fireworks. These tests include examination of chamber pressure, muzzle velocity, charge weight, muzzle flash, effect on gun wear (particularly barrel erosion), fouling of automatic and semiautomatic weapons, ignition reliability and timing, timing of maximum pressure, and overall action.[2]

---

[1]Some areas of testing were taken from presentation materials from the Sporting Arms and Ammunition Manufacturers' Institute, distributed to the committee on January 15, 1998.

[2]The tests mentioned are not a complete list of the necessary tests, but rather are offered as examples of the types of testing that any organization would need to be capable of to quantify the performance of black and smokeless powders with added markers or taggants.

Because of the specialized nature of manufacturing smokeless and black powders, all facilities that manufacture these powders also possess testing laboratories. These laboratories are used to confirm that the products meet the proper specifications. The required tests include quality (chemical and physical analyses, and thermal stability/compatibility) tests and ballistics (gun performance) testing. Few laboratories outside powder manufacturers have this same broad array of capabilities. Some may be able to carry out only the quality testing, which is chemically straightforward, while others, such as ammunition or gun producers, may have the facilities for just the ballistics tests.

REPRESENTATIVE LABORATORIES

Outside of the laboratories managed or supported by the producers and major commercial users of black and smokeless powders, most of the facilities with the relevant expertise are government owned or operated. The following list of laboratories capable of testing the effects of markers and/or taggants on propellants is representative, but not necessarily complete. The laboratories are listed for their capabilities related to quality and ballistics testing of powders.

U.S. Department of Defense

U.S. Army Research Laboratory (Aberdeen Proving Ground, MD)
U.S. Army Armament Research Development and Engineering Center (Picatinny Arsenal, Dover, NJ)
Naval Surface Warfare Center (Indian Head, MD)[3]
Naval Air Warfare Center (China Lake, CA)
Radford Army Ammunition Plant (contractor is Alliant; Radford, VA)
Lake City Army Ammunition Plant (contractor is Winchester; Independence, MO)

U.S. Department of Energy[4]

Los Alamos National Laboratory (Los Alamos, NM)[5]
Sandia National Laboratory (Albuquerque, NM)
Lawrence Livermore National Laboratory (Livermore, CA)

Canadian Government

Canadian Explosives Research Laboratory, Natural Resources Canada (Ottawa)[6]

---

[3]Committee member Ronald Simmons is affiliated with this organization.
[4]These organizations are capable of quality testing, and possibly ballistics testing.
[5]Committee member Judith Snow is affiliated with this organization.
[6]Committee member Ronald Vandebeek is affiliated with this organization.

Nonprofit Organizations

Energetic Materials Research and Testing Center, New Mexico Institute of Mining and Technology (Socorro, NM)[7]
Battelle Memorial Institute (Columbus, OH)

Private Organizations

H.P. White Laboratory (Bel Air, MD)
Stresau Laboratory, Inc. (Spooner, WI)
Pyrolabs, Inc. (Whitewater, CO)
Rho Sigma Associates, Inc. (Whitefish Bay, WI)[8]
SRI International (Menlo Park, CA)

ADDITIONAL TESTING NEEDED

Thorough examination of the inclusion of markers or taggants in black and smokeless powders requires scientific testing in areas other than quality and ballistics testing (see statement of task in Appendix B). These areas include the following:

- Utility to law enforcement (blast survivability, ease of recovery and information retrieval);
- Environmental impact (toxicity, accumulation due to legal use of powders); and
- Countermeasures (ease of removal or destruction).

While testing in these areas is important, it is not necessary for such testing to occur at the same laboratories that test the quality and performance of powders. The committee expects that further independent laboratories will be identified where these types of tests could be conducted.

---

[7]Committee member Per-Anders Persson is affiliated with this organization.
[8]Committee member Roger Schneider is affiliated with this organization.

H

Regulation of Black and Smokeless Powders

TABLE H.1 Regulation of Black and Smokeless Powders, by State

State	Does Not Regulate Purchase/ Possession	Has Some Regulation of Purchase/Possession	Exempts by Use	Exempts by Amount
ALABAMA			X	
ALASKA	X			
ARIZONA			X	
ARKANSAS	X			
CALIFORNIA[a]		Requires detailed statement from purchaser		
COLORADO			X	X
CONNECTICUT			X	X
DELAWARE				X
DISTRICT OF COLUMBIA[b]		Allows persons holding registration certificates to hand load, reload, or custom load ammunition for registered firearms		
FLORIDA				X

NOTE: The Committee on Smokeless and Black Powder would like to thank Tally Wiener, Brooklyn Law School, for her contribution to the preparation of this appendix.

State	Does Not Regulate Purchase/ Possession	Has Some Regulation of Purchase/Possession	Exempts by Use	Exempts by Amount
GEORGIA			X	X
HAWAII			X	
IDAHO			X	
ILLINOIS[c]		Allows purchase of limited quantities with identification card		
INDIANA.	X			
IOWA			X	X
KANSAS	X			
KENTUCKY			X	
LOUISIANA			X	X
MAINE				X
MARYLAND			X	X
MASSACHUSETTS[d]		Allows purchase with license or identification		
MICHIGAN[e]		Requires permit for purchase or sale		
MINNESOTA			X	
MISSISSIPPI[f]	X	Requires seller to record sale of explosives		
MISSOURI	X			
MONTANA	X			
NEBRASKA			X	
NEVADA	X			
NEW HAMPSHIRE				X

continued

TABLE H.1 Continued

State	Does Not Regulate Purchase/ Possession	Has Some Regulation of Purchase/Possession	Exempts by Use	Exempts by Amount
NEW JERSEY			X	X
NEW MEXICO			X	X
NEW YORK				X
NORTH CAROLINA	X			
NORTH DAKOTA			X	
OHIO			X	
OKLAHOMA			X	
OREGON			X	
PENNSYLVANIA			X	X
RHODE ISLAND			X	X
SOUTH CAROLINA			X	X
SOUTH DAKOTA			X	
TENNESSEE	X			
TEXAS				X
UTAH			X	
VERMONT			X	
VIRGINIA[g]		Requires person selling "explosives" to keep a record of sale		
WASHINGTON			X	X
WEST VIRGINIA			X	
WISCONSIN			X	
WYOMING	X			

NOTE: Also includes the District of Columbia. This list does not reflect (1) statutes, such as exist in a number of states, that bar purchase or possession of gunpowder by designated classes of persons, such as minors, felons, or persons addicted to, or users of, controlled substances, or (2) statutes that regulate the storage or transportation of gunpowder.

*a*See Cal. Health & Safety Code § 12102.1.
*b*See D.C. Code Ann. § 6-2341(a).
*c*See Ill. Ann. Stat. ch. 225, § 210/1004.
*d*See Mass. Gen. L. ch. 140, § 131(E).
*e*See Mich. Comp. Laws, ch. 140, § 129(C).
*f*See Miss. Code Ann. § 45-13-101.
*g*See Va. Code Ann. § 59.1-138.

SOURCE: The material in this appendix was compiled from Lexis-Nexis and WestLaw searches of each state's statutes.

I

Glossary

Acetone   A colorless flammable solvent used in the manufacture of smokeless powder and double-base propellants. Also known as dimethyl ketone.

Audit trail   A system of record keeping based on information of manufacture, distribution, and/or retail sale of a commercial product by which that product can be traced from its manufacturer to its retail purchaser.

Ball powder   Spherical smokeless powder produced by precipitation in water and flattened to various thicknesses to achieve a wide variety of ballistic performance.

Base grain   Smokeless powder that has neither a deterrent coating nor a graphite glaze.

Black powder   A deflagrating intimate physical mixture of sulfur, charcoal, and an alkali nitrate, usually potassium, but sometimes sodium nitrate.

Black powder replica   An intimate physical mixture of materials similar to those used in the manufacture of black powder designed to replace black powder in some sport-shooting applications. Compositional differences may include replacement of charcoal with compound such as sugar or ascorbic acid as fuels, and addition of other chemicals.

Bulk explosive   An unpackaged explosive that is typically shipped in trucks directly to the end user for consumption.

Caliber   Nominal bore diameter of a gun. Can be expressed in decimal inches (such as .22 caliber) or in millimeters (such as 5.56 mm).

Calorie   The unit of heat required to raise the temperature of 1 gram of water by 1 °C.

Canister   Small package of smokeless powder or black powder, typically in 1-pound, 4-pound, 5-pound, and 8-pound sizes, suitable for hand-loading and muzzle-loading purposes. The package is typically lightweight fiber or plastic construction, designed to vent quickly and prevent pressure buildup if accidentally ignited.

Cartridge-actuated device (CAD)   A self-contained device employing smokeless powder or black powder as the primary source of working gas to drive a piston to do mechanical work. Examples include air-bag-inflation devices, bomb-ejection cartridges, cable cutters, fire-extinguishing systems, parachute-release mechanisms, flight-recorder-ejection systems, and aircraft-seat-ejection units.

Centerfire   A type of small arms ammunition that uses a replaceable primer in the base of the cartridge.

Centralite   Generic name for a family of chemical stabilizers (for nitrocellulose) developed in Germany at the Central War Laboratory near Berlin about 1906.

Coincident gamma-ray emitter   A radioactive material that, upon decay, simultaneously releases two gamma rays, thereby making it detectable by use of several counters with coincident decision logic.

Combustion   A self-sustained chemical reaction with the evolution of heat and flame, proceeding at a controlled rate at considerably less than the speed of sound in the reacting medium, as opposed to the supersonic shock wave of detonation.

Commercial explosive   An explosive designed, produced, and used for commercial or industrial applications rather than for military purposes.

Comminution   The process of reducing the size of solid materials to a fine powder or dust through milling or crushing.

Compatibility   Lack of chemical reaction between a foreign material and an energetic material at elevated temperature. Normally measured by such thermal stability tests as Differential Scanning Calorimeter, Taliani Heat Test, and Vacuum Stability Test.

Composite propellant   A propellant in which the fuel and the oxidizer are separate materials, typically consisting of a blend of a crystalline oxidizer (such as sodium nitrate or ammonium perchlorate) and an amorphous or plastic fuel (such as a synthetic rubber) that acts as both fuel and binder.

Containment   The packaging required for an energetic material to explode by providing a fixed volume for the gaseous products of the combustion process. Also used in bombings to provide fragmentation designed to injure or kill bombing victims (e.g., metal pipe, polyvinyl chloride tubing, plastic bottles, or cardboard).

Corning mill   A set of calender rolls used for particle size reduction in the manufacture of black powder.

Curie   A unit of radioactivity equal to 3.7×10^{10} disintegrations per second.

Deflagration   Extremely rapid combustion, but not detonation. Sometimes used for the burning of explosive materials without the use of atmospheric oxygen.

Detection taggant   See Marker.

Deterrent   (1) Any action, process, or material that reduces the likelihood that a potential bomber will attempt an illegal bombing. (2) A surface coating applied to smokeless powder to retard the initial burning rate, initial gas generation rate, and initial flame temperature; sometimes known as a surface moderant. Typical concentrations are 1 percent to 10 percent.

Detonation   An explosive reaction initiated by a high-pressure shock wave, which propagates at a velocity higher than the speed of sound in the material and is supported by the energy released by the reaction.

Dibutyl phthalate   A colorless oily liquid commonly used as a nonenergetic plasticizer for nitrocellulose in smokeless powder.

Dinitrotoluene (DNT)   A viscous liquid nitrated product of toluene. Formerly used as a deterrent coating in smokeless powder prior to stringent restrictions in the 1980s by the U.S. Environmental Protection Agency. Not used today.

Disk powder   An extruded granule of smokeless powder that is cut as a flake and may be perforated.

Double base   Propellant or smokeless powder based on nitrocellulose and nitroglycerin as the energetic materials. Invented by Alfred Nobel in 1887. The nitroglycerin content may vary from 7 percent to 40 percent.

Ether   A colorless, highly flammable solvent used in the manufacture of smokeless powder and single-base nitrocellulose propellants. Also known as diethyl ether.

Ethyl alcohol   Grain alcohol; also known as ethanol. Colorless solvent used in the manufacture of smokeless powder and nitrocellulose-based propellants.

Ethyl centralite   A solid used as a stabilizer for nitrocellulose and smokeless powders to retard thermal decomposition and extend shelf life to several decades. In smokeless powder containing nitroglycerin, ethyl centralite is more effective than diphenylamine. Chemically known as diethyl diphenyl urea.

Exothermic   A chemical reaction that generates heat.

Explosion   A rapid expansion of matter into a volume much greater than its original volume.

Explosive material   Materials including explosives, blasting agents, and detonators. The term includes, but is not limited to, dynamite and other high explosives; slurries, emulsions, and water gels; black powder and pellet powder; initiating explosives; detonators (blasting caps); safety fuse; squibs; detonating cord; igniter cord; and igniters.

A list of explosive materials determined to be within the coverage of 18 U.S.C., Chapter 40, Importation, Manufacture, Distribution and Storage of Explosive Materials, is issued at least annually by the Director of the Bureau of Alcohol, Tobacco, and Firearms of the Department of the Treasury.

Flash suppressant   A chemical substance added to smokeless powder to reduce or eliminate visible muzzle flash.

Fragmentation   Tangible physical objects or missiles propelled outward to high speeds by an explosion, or the process in which such objects are produced. Metal, plastic, or glass pipe bomb casings can be ruptured by the high-pressure product gases of an explosive filler to produce high-speed fragments. Articles such as BBs, screws, nails, nuts and bolts, marbles, and ball bearings inside or affixed to a pipe-bomb casing are called shrapnel or langrage (also langridge) and are intended to increase the lethality of the bomb. Military bomb and warhead casings rupture in the shock front of a detonating high-explosive filler and produce very sharp, very high speed fragments, also called shrapnel. The Department of

Defense Explosive Safety Board defines a hazardous fragment as one with an impact energy of 58 foot-pounds of force (79 joules) or greater. A missile with much less kinetic energy can produce a serious injury, but it is likely that, on average, a missile impacting with 58 foot-pounds of force will ensure a casualty.

Fuel   A chemical substance requiring oxygen for complete combustion. In black powder, charcoal and sulfur are fuels.

Gamma ray   Penetrating electromagnetic radiation of very short wavelength (less than 0.1 nanometer), especially that emitted by a nucleus in a transition between two energy levels.

Glazing   The process of coating and polishing the surface of black powder and smokeless powder to improve conductivity, reduce static electricity buildup, to improve the flow properties during loading of ammunition, to increase the packing density of smokeless powder in cartridges, and to improve ignition by improving the flame spread from grain to grain.

Grain   Term used to describe a definite geometrical shape of smokeless powder or black powder; often confused with a unit of weight where 1 pound is equal to 7,000 grains.

Half-life   The time required for the intensity of a radioactive material to decrease to one-half its initial value.

Hand loading   (Also known as reloading) The process of reusing cartridge cases repeatedly with new charges of smokeless powder, primer, and bullet (projectile). The cartridges are loaded individually by hand, and used repeatedly before discarding for the purposes of reducing cost or manipulating ballistic performance.

Hangfire   A noticeable delay in ammunition that occurs after a primer fires, and before the propellant charge ignites. In some instances, the delay may be several seconds or longer.

High explosive   An explosive characterized by a very high rate of reaction, development of high pressure, and the presence of a detonation wave in the explosion.

Identification taggant   See Taggant.

Improvised explosive   Explosive material that was not manufactured commercially.

Improvised explosive device   A mechanism such as a pipe bomb fabricated from explosive, commercial, or homemade materials.

IMR   A single-base smokeless powder, originally produced by DuPont, and known as improved military rifle powder. IMR powders are now produced by Expro in Valleyfield, Quebec, Canada. Characterized as a single-perforated cylinder with a deterrent coating.

Inert   Nonreactive or nondetonable. Some ingredients of smokeless powder are referred to as inert, meaning that they contribute no energy but are consumed during combustion.

Initiator   Represents a broad spectrum of small devices that function either by mechanical or electrical impulse and that are used to provide a flame for propellants or a detonation wave for explosives. An initiator can be a detonator, detonation cord, or similar device used to start detonation or deflagration in an explosive material. When used with smokeless powder or black powder, an initiator produces a flame used to start combustion and normally does not produce detonation.

Joule   A unit of energy approximately equal to 0.239 calories.

Lift charge   Granulated black powder used to propel aerial display fireworks into the air. The burning characteristics of black powder substitutes and smokeless powders make them unsuitable for use as lift charges.

Low explosive   A commonly used term for propellants, or explosives designed to burn rather than detonate.

Magazine   A building or structure used to store explosives, smokeless powder, or black powder.

Marker   A material (or tracer element) added to explosives that can be sensed by an associated detection instrument. Explosives that contain such a marker are considered "marked."

Mesh   Refers to the screen or sieve size, as measured by the diameter of the opening. For example, 30 mesh is equivalent to 600 microns.

Methyl centralite   A solid chemical used as a stabilizer for nitrocellulose and smokeless powders to retard thermal decomposition, chemically known as dimethyl diphenyl urea.

Micron   A unit of length defined as 1×10^{-6} meters.

Muzzle loading   The process of using black powder (or a black powder substitute) in a gun designed solely for black powder. Such guns can only be loaded from the muzzle and are not capable of withstanding the high pressures generated by smokeless powder. Such muzzle loaders are common in Civil War reenactments and are not classed as firearms.

Nitrocellulose (NC)   An energetic fibrous polymer derived from the nitration of cellulose and characterized primarily by the degree of nitration. Smokeless powder typically uses nitrocellulose of 13.1 percent to 13.3 percent nitrogen, where the theoretical maximum nitrogen content is 14.14 percent.

Nitroglycerin (NG)   An energetic colorless liquid manufactured by the nitration of synthetic or natural glycerin. Used to plasticize nitrocellulose in double- and triple-base propellants.

Nitroguanidine (NQ)   A moderately energetic solid incorporated in some propellants as a coolant and flash suppressant to produce with nitroglycerine and nitrocellulose a triple-base propellant. Not normally found in commercial smokeless powders.

Nonideal explosive   An explosive that releases its energy slowly following shock compression and heating. It usually exhibits thicker reaction zones and contributes a smaller fraction of its total energy toward supporting the shock wave.

Opacifier   Used in smokeless powder to prevent radiant energy (during combustion) from penetrating the surface and producing wormholing. Typically, carbon black is used for this purpose at a concentration of 0.1 percent to 0.5 percent.

Original equipment manufacturer (OEM)   As used in this report, OEM refers to the commercial ammunition manufacturer that loads smokeless powder into cartridges.

Oxidizer   A chemical that yields oxygen to promote the combustion of a fuel. In black powder, potassium nitrate is an oxidizer.

Oxygen balance   The amount of oxygen in excess of that required for complete combustion of carbon to carbon dioxide and hydrogen to water, expressed as a weight percent or grams of oxygen per 100 grams of material. A negative oxygen balance, as found in most smokeless powders, denotes a deficiency of oxygen after combustion.

Packaged explosive   An explosive material manufactured, sold, and used in the form of individual cartridges or containers.

Pipe bomb   A type of improvised explosive device containing an energetic material filler (most commonly, but not necessarily propellant) enclosed by metal, polyvinyl chloride, cardboard, or other material cylinders, often with additional fragmentation devices for increased antipersonnel effect.

Plasticizer   A liquid that dissolves or swells a polymer to impart better processability, to waterproof the propellant, reduce brittleness, and tailor the energy level. Plasticizer can act either as a coolant or a source of energy. Typically used at a concentration of 2 percent to 40 percent.

Polyvinyl chloride   A common industrial and household plastic used primarily in piping.

Precursor chemical   A chemical used to synthesize an explosive material through a chemical process or as a component in a mixture that enhances the destructive force.

Primer   A small initiating device used to ignite smokeless or black powder. Can function by the stimulus of either mechanical action or electrical discharge. Typically, primers are located in the base of the cartridge case and are replaceable after firing.

Propellant   A chemical mixture such as black or smokeless powder that burns in the absence of atmospheric oxygen at a self-sustaining, exothermic, controlled subsonic rate, generating heat and gas, and capable of performing mechanical work.

Propellant-actuated device (PAD)   See Cartridge-actuated device.

Pyrotechnic composition   A mixture of chemical compounds and/or elements which is capable upon ignition of a self-contained and self-sustained exothermic reaction, for the production of heat, light, sound, gas, smoke, and/or motion.

Reloading   See Hand loading.

Residue   Any energetic material that has not been completely consumed in the intended application and can be recovered for laboratory analysis.

Rework   The process of recycling material in manufacturing operations to eliminate waste and scrap, which otherwise would require open burning or disposal.

Rework from partially processed material is recycled to the beginning step of the manufacturing.

Rimfire   A low-cost small-arms cartridge (usually .22 caliber) with the priming compound contained in the rim. Because the cartridge is deformed during firing, it cannot be reloaded. As opposed to centerfire, which has a cavity for a replaceable primer.

Rolling   A process of size reduction during the manufacture of smokeless powder, in which the propellant is passed between a pair of rolls (also known as calender rolls used in papermaking) separated by a very small adjustable space.

Saltpeter   Potassium nitrate.

Shock wave   A high-pressure wave or pressure disturbance traveling at a speed faster than sound in that medium.

Single base   Smokeless powder or propellant based solely on nitrocellulose as the energetic material.

Small arms   Guns, typically handheld, or ammunition for a gun, of less than 20-mm caliber.

Smokeless powder   A granular, free-flowing, solid propellant of various morphologies, using nitrocelluse as an active ingredient. It is classified as single base (with nitrocelluse as the only active ingredient), double base (with nitrocelluse and nitroglycerin), or triple base (with nitrocelluse, nitroglycerin, and nitroguanidine). Smokeless powder is commonly used in small-arms ammunition.

Solvent recovery   The process of capturing, recovery, and reuse of volatile, flammable processing solvents used in the manufacture of smokeless powder to avoid discharging the solvents into the atmosphere.

Solve rate   The percentage of bombing incidents for which a perpetrator can be identified.

Stabilizer   A chemical incorporated in solid propellant to react with the decomposition products and prolong the shelf life of the propellant. Typically used at concentration of 0.5 percent to 2 percent. When properly stabilized, smokeless powder has a shelf life of nearly 100 years at 20 °C.

Taggant   An additive (or tracer element) designed to survive an explosion and to be recoverable at the bomb scene, used to aid law enforcement personnel in either tracing explosive materials to the last legal purchaser or to provide evidence against a known suspect.

Torr   A unit of measure for pressure, approximately equal to 0.02 pounds per square inch, or 133 pascals. Standard atmospheric pressure is 760 torr.

Tracing   The process of identifying a commercial product by use of an external agent and record keeping through the manufacturing, distribution, and sale of that product.

Triple base   Solid propellant containing nitrocellulose, nitroglycerin (or, e.g. diglycol dinitrate), and nitroguanidine.

Tubular powder   An extruded form of smokeless powder cut into rods whose length either equals or exceeds their diameter. Most, but not all, examples will have a central perforation and will possess fairly uniform dimensions of length and diameter.

Vapor pressure   The pressure exerted by the vapor phase of a chemical in equilibrium with its solid or liquid phase.

Vinsol resin   A naturally occurring thermoplastic resin, extracted along with turpentine from tree stumps, and used in smokeless powder as a deterrent coating.

Web   The smallest dimension of a smokeless powder granule.

J

Acronyms and Abbreviations

ANFO	Ammonium nitrate/fuel oil
ATF	Alcohol, Tobacco, and Firearms, Bureau of
CMA	Chemical Manufacturers Association
DMNB	2,3-dimethyl-2,3-dinitrobutane
DNT	Dinitrotoluene
EGDN	Ethylene glycol dinitrate
FAA	Federal Aviation Administration
FBI	Federal Bureau of Investigation
ICAO	International Civil Aviation Organization
IED	Improvised explosive device
LOVA	Low vulnerability ammunition (powders)
3M	Minnesota Mining and Manufacturing Company
MNT	Mononitrotoluene
NC	Nitrocellulose
NG	Nitroglycerine
NQ	Nitroguanidine
OEM	Original equipment manufacturer
OTA	Office of Technology Assessment
PEL	Permissible exposure limit
PVC	Polyvinyl chloride